Susan Hawthorne is the author of four books of non-fiction, three works of fiction and nine collections of poetry as well ten edited anthologies. *Bibliodiversity* (2014) has been translated into five languages, *Wild Politics* (2002) has been published in India, and *The Spinifex Quiz Book* (1993) has been translated into two languages. She has been active in the women's liberation movement since 1973, was involved in Melbourne's Rape Crisis Centre and performed as an aerialist in two women's circuses. Her two most recent books are *The Sacking of the Muses* (2019, poetry) and *Dark Matters: A novel* (2017). She has taught English to Arabic-speaking women, worked in Aboriginal education and has taught across a number of subject areas in universities. She is Adjunct Professor in the School of Humanities at James Cook University, Townsville. She was the winner of the 2017 Penguin Random House Best Achievement in Writing in the Inspire Awards for her work increasing people's awareness of epilepsy and the politics of disability.

Other books by Susan Hawthorne

non-fiction
Bibliodiversity: A Manifesto for Independent Publishing (2014)
Wild Politics: Feminism, Globalisation and Bio/diversity (2002)
The Spinifex Quiz Book: A Book of Women's Answers (1993)

fiction
Dark Matters: A Novel (2017)
Limen (2013, verse novel)
The Falling Woman (1992/2004)

poetry
The Sacking of the Muses (2019)
Lupa and Lamb (2014)
Valence: Considering War through Poetry and Theory (2011, chapbook)
Cow (2011)
Earth's Breath (2009)
Unsettling the Land (with Suzanne Bellamy, 2008, chapbook)
The Butterfly Effect (2005)
Bird and Other Writings on Epilepsy (1999)
The Language in My Tongue (1993)

anthologies
Lesbian Poets and Writers: Live Encounters (2018)
Horse Dreams: The Meaning of Horses in Women's Lives
    (with Jan Fook and Renate Klein, 2004)
Cat Tales: The Meaning of Cats in Women's Lives
    (with Jan Fook and Renate Klein, 2003)
September 11, 2001: Feminist Perspectives (with Bronwyn Winter, 2002)
Cyberfeminism: Connectivity, Critique and Creativity (with Renate Klein, 1999)
Car Maintenance, Explosives and Love and Other Lesbian Writings
    (with Cathie Dunsford and Susan Sayer, 1997)
Australia for Women: Travel and Culture (with Renate Klein, 1994)
Angels of Power and Other Reproductive Creations (with Renate Klein, 1991)
The Exploding Frangipani: Lesbian Writing from Australia and New Zealand
    (with Cathie Dunsford, 1990)
Moments of Desire: Sex and Sexuality by Australian Feminist Writers
    (with Jenny Pausacker, 1989)
Difference: Writings by Women (1985)

In Defence
of Separatism

Susan Hawthorne

First published by Spinifex Press, 2019

Spinifex Press Pty Ltd
PO Box 5270, North Geelong, VIC 3215, Australia
PO Box 105, Mission Beach, QLD 4852, Australia

women@spinifexpress.com.au
www.spinifexpress.com.au

Cover design by Deb Snibson, MAPG
Typesetting by Helen Christie, Blue Wren Books
Typeset in Utopia
Printed by McPherson's Printing Group

 A catalogue record for this
book is available from the
National Library of Australia

ISBN: 9781925950045 (paperback)
ISBN: 9781925950052 (eBook)

For women with courage

Contents

Acknowledgements

1976

This text was originally submitted as an Honours thesis in Philosophy at La Trobe University. I would like to thank my supervisor Anna Cushan for helpful criticisms and suggestions through the year. I would also like to thank Sue Ivanyi for the many valuable discussions we have had in various aspects of the thesis. Thanks also go to Helen Lang, Lin Cooper, Amanda Ressom and Jen Feret; and to Gay Dunn for typing the original thesis.

2019

In 2012, Kathleen Barry commented on the text and assisted in helping me think through some of the challenges. My thanks to all the feminists who have contributed to the debates over more than forty years and to those who continue the struggle now. Thanks to Deb Snibson and Helen Christie for fast work on the cover and text respectively. To Estelle Disch for her beautiful cover art. And to all at Spinifex Pauline Hopkins, Maralann Damiano, Rachael McDiarmid and Caitlin Roper.

I would like to thank many courageous radical feminists who had stood up to protest proposed changes in the law. This has been a particularly vicious fight in English speaking countries. A significant number of women's organisations and individuals have engaged with these important but difficult arguments, including with gung-ho governments changing laws — laws that erase women's life experiences and deny women access to spaces of our own — almost always without consultation with women.

To Renate Klein, I cannot express enough thanks for the years of conversations. Without our intense and ongoing discussions about everything under the sun over more than three decades, my life would be much the poorer.

Preface 2019

It's a long time since this thesis was first written. Since 1976 I have benefited from conversations with numerous feminists on this subject: some friendly, some not so.

When I wrote this thesis, I was punished academically for it. It was departmental policy to choose the examiners: one was my supervisor, the second was a philosopher with whom I had argued about rape. He told me that being raped was no different from being mugged. The low grade I was given was very likely due to him. It was sufficiently low to ensure I would not be able to continue to postgraduate level in philosophy. This was forty years before #MeToo, my chances of having it reconsidered were zilch. I had no witness to the conversation about rape and he was popular in the department. I attempted to have it published in feminist journals, but was unsuccessful. In 1982, there was an international call for papers on the topic of separatism. I heard about it and sent it off to Sarah Hoagland and Julia Penelope. I heard nothing. Some time later I heard that the anthology *For Lesbians Only* was to be published but that no essays from Australia were to be included. The only essays accepted were from North America and France. This has long struck me as an unfortunate basis for accepting work for an anthology. Either one is clear from the start about the parameters, or else the editors should make (often difficult) decisions based on quality. Perhaps my essay would still not have been published in that important anthology, but at least it would not have left the Australian lesbians who had sent their work off in good faith reeling from this rationale. In 1990, I was lucky enough to get a shortened and edited version published in *Feminist Knowledge Reader* (edited by Sneja Gunew, Routledge, London). That version was rather eviscerated and considerably shorter. In 2019, that version will be published in *Oslobodjenje lezbejki: feministicki tekstovi* (1968–1980): *Lesbian Liberation: Feminist Articles (1968–1980)* edited by Nela Pamukovic, Zagreb, Croatia and Milos Urosevic, Belgrade, Serbia. This book is almost the same as the original with a few edits, corrections and the odd improvement in argument. I have also added footnotes (in italics) where the historical or current situations warrant commentary.

The title of my thesis was suggested by Robert Paul Wolff's small book, *In Defense of Anarchism* (1970). I was creating a theoretical history for my ideas about separatism within the boundaries of political philosophy. Feminist ideas were hotly debated and almost everyone I knew at that time had at least a nodding acquaintance with Marxist theory. I certainly did and had studied Political Philosophy, Marxism, Feminism (all Philosophy subjects) as well as Revolutionary History, African History and Women's History in the years leading up to writing my thesis. I was also active in a number of feminist campaigns and organisations, among them: volunteer at Women's Liberation Centre (1974–1975); Halfway House (Melbourne's first women's refuge, 1975); Rape Crisis Centre (Melbourne's first, 1974–1976). I attended conferences, women's dances, and various events in the arts, especially theatre which had a vibrant Melbourne scene. I listened to bands like ClitOris (from Sydney), Women's Electric Band (WEB, from Melbourne), The Shameless Hussies (Adelaide), Ovarian Sisters (Hobart). I went to picnics and ate at the No Men, No Meat Restaurant. It was a time where women were experimenting with the boundaries of the possible. I knew women who had taken up residence on Amazon Acres[1], The Woman's Land and Herland in New South Wales[2] and heard stories from women returning from the Michigan Womyn's Music Festival which ran annually from 1976–2015. I also read utopian women's fiction.

Times have changed and with the advent of postmodernism in the 1980s and its increasing influence in academic discourse, including queer theory, the idea of separatism went underground though many feminists practised it in their lives. The punishment for writing about separatism in 1976 was exclusion from academia and publishing; in 2019, it is more likely to attract both virtual and real attack on social media and in intellectual circles.[3] But the topic is now under discussion with events being held to discuss the issue of women's separate

---

1   *For Australian fictional representations see Moorhead 1987/2011; 1991/2002; 2000.*

2   *ABC Radio National has two programs about the women's lands: Part 1 on 30 July 2019: <https://radio.abc.net.au/programitem/pexQXXyBdQ> and Part 2 on 6 August 2019 <https://www.abc.net.au/radionational/programs/ the-history-listen/amazon-acres-sisterhood-under-siege/11251542>*

3   *Journalist, Meghan Murphy, who runs the Canadian online site Feminist Current, was permanently banned from Twitter in 2018 for referring to a male-born transgender with the pronoun 'he'. (Murphy 2019a).*

spaces. Questioning women for wanting to run women-only events only occurs when men want to colonise women's energy and activism.

While this is not a book about the transgender debate, the politics of self-identification laws which are being proposed, developed, or are under review in many westernised countries are connected to the arguments outlined in this book and go to the heart of whether women are an oppressed sex who, in order to have safe places, do need rooms of our own (Lawford-Smith 2019).

A note on language

The language I use in this book is the language of feminist politics in 1976. It is quite different from today's political language and in the intervening years it is something I have thought about a lot. As a poet, as someone keenly interested in words and languages, words matter to me.

Sex is the term I use when speaking about women and men, boys and girls. I acknowledge that there are intersex people and there are people who feel uncomfortable with the culture and expectations of their sex, most of these people call themselves transgender or non-binary. Female is a biological status indicated by an XX chromosome. Woman is a noun that refers to adult human females with XX chromosomes in their DNA.

Sex is a political term and as a 1970s feminist, it was the sex class of women that impassioned me and the women of the Women's Liberation Movement to rebel against the expectations of sex role stereotypes. These sex role stereotypes were based on our biological sex. Women's biological sex includes the capacity to give birth (not every woman needs to give birth for this to be true); women, those with XX chromosomes have a vagina, uterus, ovaries, produce eggs, and have breasts (even when these parts malfunction or are missing they remain biological women). Sex is not an identity, it is an integral part of our bodies. Or as one Facebook meme puts it: "sex is why women are oppressed; gender is how women are oppressed."

Gender was a term that Ann Oakley began to use in 1972 and she used it to refer to the way in which sex role stereotypes were used to socialise girls and boys into being 'feminine' and 'masculine'. Up until this time gender was only used as a grammatical term to identify nouns in Indo-European languages like French, Sanskrit, Greek, etc. Nouns are masculine, feminine, neuter. Gender in its social use as defined by Anne Oakley meant feminine and masculine but the social traits — feminine and masculine — are extreme forms of behaviour expressed by women and men. They are sex-role stereotypes and prescriptive rather than descriptive. It is these prescriptive behaviours and qualities that are most frequently taken up as 'norms' by transgender individuals. And they are the qualities espoused by transgender organisations and activists.

Masculine refers to behaviour considered strong, heroic, energetic, ambitious and is almost always seen to be a positive quality in spite of the fact that masculinity is also brutal, violent and aggressive. Feminine refers to the domestic sphere and is associated with the passive, gentle, nurturing, emotional, hysterical and is almost always considered to be negative despite the fact that femininity is also associated with compassion, beauty, and empathy — all qualities required for social cohesion. Biology was something I had seen before my eyes growing up on a farm. The word neutered was used to refer to rams that had been castrated, but they were still male; just as a steer remains male but is not a bull. What is a distinctive difference between gender-critical feminists and transgenders and their apologists is that the former do not abide by these prescriptive qualities while the latter valorise them.

Over the last two decades[4] there has been a considerable shift in the language usage. Almost no one these days knows the difference between sex and gender, even editors. A novel I read three years ago has a character speaking in 1951 using the word 'gender'. It simply could not have happened. Another couple of clear examples of inappropriate use: in books on archaeology I see an increasing number of writers using the word gender in relation to bodies found at archaeological sites. There is no way the researcher can know how the person expressed his or her sex that long ago. Have you heard people asking about the gender of your baby or your dog? Again, this use is incorrect because the baby doesn't yet know and the dog couldn't care less. I use the word sex when talking about women and men; I use the word gender when discussing grammar or when it is used in a quotation.

---

4   *Janice Raymond's critique,* The Transsexual Empire *was published in 1979 and for a long time was the only book to offer a critique of this shift in language and politics.*

Gender became popular alongside post-modernism and queer politics, neither of which has advanced feminism. The sex class of women is what feminists are fighting on behalf of. The transgender and queer post-modernists are fighting for something different. Feminists want to get rid of gender; transgender and queer post-modernists want to reify gender; they want to be positive about the expression of feminine gender. The stereotypes that are put forward by trans activists are the very same ones we were trying to overcome in the 1970s. The claim for inclusiveness is a false one since under this supposedly inclusive mantra women are excluded. Here are a few examples:

- In 2015, a women's group at the University of Auckland organised a day in which female students could 'ice your own vagina' and drink 'pussy tails'. This was intended as a way of encouraging women students to develop a positive relationship with their bodies. The women in this group were accused of perpetrating hatred against trans people because cupcakes were regarded as non-inclusive. One commentator went as far as saying they were 'killing' transpeople though this action.

- The language for women's bodies is being erased. You can no longer breastfeed, you must chest feed; maternity hospitals are pushed to use terms like pregnant people and even the word mother is problematised. The vagina has been renamed the 'front hole'. The proposed new law on abortion in NSW (2019) uses the language of pregnant persons instead of pregnant women.

- More extreme language practices are prescribed when speaking about lesbians (remember lesbians are women who want to have sex with women): lesbians who do not want to have sex with individuals who say they are women but have a penis are accused of having erected a 'cotton ceiling'. Lesbians are then blamed, rather than those trying to impose colonising linguistic change.

- Women's human rights are under attack as when Jessica (previously Johnathan) Yaniv asked a Muslim woman and dozens of others to provide a Brazilian wax on his genitals — penis, testicles and all — they refused and had human rights complaints filed against them. Some of the women have lost their businesses (Murphy 2019b).

- Radical feminists who continue to use words like woman are said to be TERFS (Trans Exclusive Radical Feminists) or SWERFS (Sex Work Exclusive Radical Feminists). This is hate speech against women. In London in 2018, the slogan 'Repeat after me, Trans women are women' was projected on the Justice Ministry building [5] (Duffy 2018). Resistance to this has created a counter slogan 'Women: adult human female' which has been used by radical feminists in demonstrations and across social media platforms.

- Any woman who continues to use the term woman without queering it or giving it a non-binary twist is told that she is a cis-woman. The word cis is most easily explained with an

---

5   *The phrase 'Repeat after me' is ominously like George Orwell's Ministry of Truth in his novel,* 1984. *The purpose of the Ministry of Truth was as a propaganda machine for spreading lies that purport to be truths.*

alpine analogy: trans-alpine means across the mountains; cis-alpine means this side of the mountains. Anyone, therefore who feels positive about the word woman is called cis. Interestingly, there appear to be many more cis-women than cis-men in the world. This might indicate that it is those born male who now want to cross the mountain are the ones imposing the language change. Is this any different from mansplaining?

This is only part of the language wars. There have also been physical attacks on women's centres and against women by trans activists. The Vancouver Rape Crisis Centre had to go to court to defend its right to decide on who should be on their collective and in 2019 their funding has been discontinued. Hate-filled trolling on the Internet is a regular occurrence; and public spaces such as the San Francisco Library have been used to hold exhibitions of work that vilifies women, especially radical feminists and lesbians; lesbians are no longer welcome at Pride Marches, instead groups of trans activists and trans supporters wear T-shirts like I PUNCH TERFS; and in the UK, 60-year-old Maria MacLauchlan was assaulted by a trans-identified male who calls himself Tara Wolf (Murphy 2018).

In Glasgow, Scotland in August 2018, a rape crisis centre was defunded because it was set up to deal with the rape of women and girls. My involvement in feminist activism extends back to 1974 when I was a volunteer at Melbourne Rape Crisis Centre when it first opened. Only women rang to report rape. Only women established and ran the centre. Men who want help after being raped should be able to be assisted not by women in women-run rape crisis centres, but in other centres or by professionals with the required training. As Judith Herman has written about the process of trauma and recovery, there should be

> a gradual shift from unpredictable danger to reliable safety, from dissociated trauma to acknowledged memory and from stigmatized isolation to restored social connection (Herman 1992, p. 155).

Women attending a rape crisis centre are still experiencing 'unpredictable danger' and so the presence of men can trigger symptoms of PTSD.

When a political group wants to strategise so that its members can arrive at agreed-on political tactics and ideas, they call for, and create, separate spaces. These might be in coffee shops, in community centres, in one another's homes or in semi-public spaces such as workers clubs, even cinemas. When the proletariat was rebelling, they did not ask the capitalists and aristocracy to join them (even if a few did); when the civil rights movement started it was not thanks to the ideas and politics of white people (even though some whites joined to support the cause); when the women's liberation movement sprang into life, it was women joining together to fight against their oppression.

The difference is that women are supposed to love men. And while there may well be love across classes and ethnic groups, religions and languages, there is not an expectation that this should happen. In the case of women, this expectation remains no matter how tolerant a society claims to be. These arguments would not be so intense if trans people were supporting women (and some do), but most seem intent on undermining feminist actions and the need for women to be able to have gatherings without men present (whether transitioning or not).

The word 'identity' is also problematic. In the 1970s we spoke of political causes and of collective action. Today, the term 'gender identity' is the most frequent use of this word, but it is used more and more in popular culture. If I say my identity is female, I am speaking about a biological reality. If I say my identity is Australian, that's not the only facet of me. Identity individualises people and disconnects the parts of people. My identity is neither Australian nor female, nor white, nor a person with a disability, nor lesbian, nor a member of the over 60 group, nor a rural person, nor poet, nor any other aspect of my life. Identity does nothing to help people join forces for a political purpose. If I imagine that I am a rich white man, will I suddenly become rich or male? I think not.

Many of us have to fill in forms and these days they are mostly online. On paper forms it used to be possible to cross out the word 'gender' and write 'sex', but with online forms this is no longer an option. Forms, especially census and other government forms, are a way of gauging what services need to be provided to whom and in what regions. The census relies on an assumption of honesty, but if we no longer understand our language and no longer know that sex means woman and man, and gender means socially constructed behaviour, we are not going to have very accurate data on which to base policies and services. Identity, therefore, is not a useful political term because 'identity' dissects and disconnects us. It makes collective action impossible and reifies individualism. It also creates false statistics with an apparent rise in violent crimes by women — transwomen — who for statistical purposes are counted as women.

Separatism, as a strategy, has been developed by many oppressed peoples. In the 1970s, it was picked up by radical feminists. The ideas set out below come out of that period but are just as relevant today given the attempts at creating new laws which not only impinge on the human rights of women, but are also creating a view of the world which does not reflect reality. From mastectomies undergone by young lesbians who feel uncomfortable in their female bodies; to children as young as 10–12 taking puberty blocker drugs, and from 14–16 taking cross-sex hormones that will affect their lives for ever and having deleterious health outcomes; to women facing physical violence and legal threats, it seems that the time has come to put out into the public sphere the ideas developed here.

In the text that follows, original footnotes from 1976 are in roman typeface while footnotes in italics indicate that they have been added specifically for this 2019 edition.

Statement of the Argument

Working assumption
We live in a patriarchal society in which inequality between men and women is institutionalised.

'Power' (the word) as used here is a generic term for a set of relations of varying effectiveness, i.e. it names the relations. Within the seven forms of power which I identify, I discuss the following features:

- Most women have access to fewer forms of power, the forms accessible are the less effective forms, and less effectiveness can be achieved within those forms.
- Most men have access to more forms of power, the forms accessible are the more effective forms of power, and more effectiveness can be achieved within those forms.
- Most men have access to more, and more effective forms of power than most women.
- Most relations between men and women are unequal.
- Because most men have more access to more, and more effective forms of power, all men *can* oppress all women.
- Ease of access to forms of power determines exercise of power.
- Most women can only exercise limited forms of power, those exercised are mostly the less effective forms of power, and the power exercised within those forms are limited.

- Most men can exercise extensive forms of power, they can exercise the more effective forms of power, and the power exercised within those forms is more extensive.
- Oppression in a patriarchy is the systematic exercise of power by men.
- Most men do exercise power over women.
- Some men oppress most women, some men oppress all women, and most men oppress some women.
- Institutions created by powerful men give legitimacy to the oppression of women.
- Ideology provides rationales for oppression.
- Heterosexuality limits legitimate personal relations to relations between men and women.
- Heterosexuality is an institution.
- Relations between men and women are unequal in power.
- Therefore heterosexual relations are unequal in power.
- The institution of heterosexuality offers women inducements for remaining in it and/or deprivation for stepping outside it and/or promises of benefits and/or threats of deprivation.
- The inducements are not as great as they appear to be.
- The actual deprivations are not as great as they appear to be.
- Women gain in the short term by partaking in heterosexuality.
- Women gain in the long run by stepping outside the institution of heterosexuality.
- The opportunities for stepping outside the heterosexual mode of relating are few.
- There exist few alternative modes of relating outside the institution of heterosexuality.

- Feminism offers women an alternative mode of relating.
- Feminism offers women an opportunity to step outside the institution of heterosexuality.
- Relations between women are less likely to be unequal in power (than relations between men and women).
- Relations between feminists are even less likely to be unequal in power.
- Relations between feminists are strategically important to achieve political goals.
- Separatism minimises the extent to which men can exercise power over women.
- Not being systematically involved in unequal power relations provides a better basis for effective political action.
- Separatism is a viable strategy for women's liberation.

Chapter 1
Introduction

1.1 Power

'Power' names a set of relations that pertain in a given situation. Social power is the set of relations that pertain between persons or groups of persons. It

> ... is usually a reciprocal process among all participants, and is rarely determined by a single actor no matter how unequal the situation might appear (Olsen 1970, p. 3).

That is, each individual within the relation contributes to the eventual power differential. The differential that results may be affected by external factors such as social conditioning, economic resources and physical strength.

A group may be considered dominant if that group is advantaged in their ease of access to power and thus in their opportunity to exercise power. This allows the members of that group greater opportunity in the development of their individual and collective potential. In a patriarchy it is predominantly men who are advantaged in these ways while women are systematically disallowed opportunities which would enable them easy access to and exercise of many of the forms of power, and to the effective forms of power.

Power relations vary in intensity, stability and effectiveness according to the nature of the relations between the persons involved and the context in which it occurs. When the relations are between men and women, men have the greater chance of success because they have access to more effective forms of power. Power relations are almost always weighted in the man's favour and so relations between men and women may be said to be power-based relations. Relations between persons where the power is not consistently weighted in one person's favour are not power-based relations. This is not to deny that there is a relation of power between the persons, but it means that the relation is not based on one person consistently having power over the other based on their sex.

In order to spell out the ways in which sex-power relations may vary according to the nature of the persons involved — and the context — and to show how it is that women generally have access to and exercise of a limited range of power, but generally only to the least effective forms, I use the classification of seven forms of power identified by de Crespigny (1970).

My use of the letters A and B may be taken to refer to individuals or groupings of individuals.

Coercive power

Exercising coercive power requires using or threatening to use one's access to power that allows the exercise of power which leads to agent B complying with agent A to meet A's desired end. For coercion to be successful A's opportunity of access to forms of power must be greater than B's or B must believe they are greater, and further B must have complied with A. B may comply without coercion actually being exercised if B believes A's access to power to be greater and the reason that she will be better off by complying than by resisting. This belief may be based on past experience or on a rational judgement of the chance of successful resistance (or weighing up the consequences).

Coercion does not always involve physical force. Instead B may be deprived of access to social, economic or emotional support thereby diminishing B's chances of successful resistance to A.

Coercive power must be intended at some time by A, but neither A nor B needs to know it is being exercised at a particular time. This is because included within its scope are *threats* of coercion as well as actual *instances* of coercion.

In the case of relations between men and women, the following is an example of an actual instance of the exercise of coercive power, as well as its exercise and expectation of further instances of its exercise.

> We all know stories about husbands beating up their wives after the party when they have reached the privacy of their home. Many of us have experienced at least a few blows from husbands or lovers when we refuse to submit to them. It is difficult to assess the frequency of physical attacks within so-called love relationships, because women rarely tell even one another when they have taken place. By developing a complicated ethic of loyalty (described above in terms of privacy) men have protected themselves from such reports leaking out and becoming public information. Having already been punched for stepping out of the role, the woman is more than a little reluctant to tell anyone of the punishment because it would

violate the loyalty code which is an even worse infraction of the rules and most likely would result in further and perhaps more severe punishment (Gillespie citing O'Connor 1975, p. 78).

Each time the man is successful in his exercise of power, his access to further instances of this exercise is increased. He thus becomes cumulatively more effective in his exercise and gains more access to other forms of power. The woman's access to and exercise of power on the other hand is diminished and she is rendered cumulatively less effective.

Inducive power
He may gain, for instance, by increasing his access to inducive power. Inducive power is exercised when B complies with A's wishes because she believes that she will benefit by complying. Inducements may take the form of rewards and/or withdrawal of threats and/or instances of deprivation. B may act in compliance with A given the inducements, when she might not have in the event that they were not offered.

Social conflict is absent when inducive power is exercised. If conflict is present then it is an instance of coercive power by threat or belief of threat. Inducive power entails gains for B or the belief of gains for B. B may not in fact gain by complying but believes she will. Thus inducive power, though apparently beneficial to B is inconsistent with B's autonomy, but not necessarily with B's liberty in the negative sense. Apologists of inducive power will argue that B made a decision to comply.

For example, the security of marriage is an inducement offered to most people, particularly women. It is an inducement because women can improve their social status by marrying a man of higher status (but even when this is not the case a bad marriage might be considered better than no marriage). Marriage is a goal aspired to by many women because they believe they will benefit in some way.

The inducements are not always empty. Some women do benefit in the short term by marrying: this may be by acquiring a modicum of security and/or social respect.

However, marriage is inconsistent with women's autonomy in the long term. Take for example the naming convention, unchallenged until recently,[6] applied to married women. A woman who marries Jim Brown becomes Mrs Jim Brown — without reference to the woman herself, only to the man to whom she is married. She relinquishes her autonomy and her identity in this sphere.

Power of this sort is an activity intended, though not all the attendant implications need be intended.

Reactional power

There are forms of power which do not rely on intentions to affect individual behaviour but which do affect behaviour because of the way in which person B reacts to A because of her beliefs about A and because B believes that she will benefit in some way by acting in accordance with her belief.

It applies also to institutions, especially where B is a subordinate of A and refrains from certain activities because of the effect it may have on her chances of promotion.

---

6   *I am referring here to the early 1970s.*

An exercise of reactional power occurs unknown to A, particularly when B's beliefs about A's reactions lead him [her] to abstain from what [she] he would otherwise have done (de Crespigny 1970, pp. 47–8).

Reactional power '... is a function of B's beliefs about A's reactions' (de Crespigny 1970, p. 47).

... unlike the previous forms of power [the] effects are always prospective. Where harmful effects are feared they may be such as to deprive B or another of something [she] he has or of something [she] he expects to have (de Crespigny 1970, p. 47).

An example of reactional power is heterosexuality. Most people in our society are, or claim to be, heterosexual. The society tends not to see this as problematic, partly because the body politic assumes that it is 'natural'. Moreover, homosexual members of the society are systematically subjected to the findings of certain psychologists and psychiatrists and the like in their endeavours to 'cure' non-heterosexual people. Further, many countries still retain legislation which prohibits certain sexual activities which lie outside the domain of male-female relationships. This results in some non-heterosexual people acting in accordance with the heterosexual norm publicly because they believe that the reactions of heterosexual people could deprive them of their freedom to otherwise associate with whom they choose.[7]

---

7   *It was not until 1994 that the Commonwealth of Australia legalised sexual activity (in private). Some states passed similar earlier laws (South Australia, 1972), some later (Tasmania 1997).*

Impedimental power

Reactional power can on occasion become impedimental power, as would be the case in the above example if a person is not promoted because of their sexual preference. Impedimental power differs from reactional power because the latter is B centred. B decides, according to the available information, what she thinks A's reaction will be and on that basis behaves accordingly. Impedimental power, by contrast, is A centred, A makes the decisions.

Impedimental power is a deliberate manipulation of obstacles by A in order to prevent B from attaining some desired goal. It is closely related to coercive power because it is deliberate on A's part, and limits B's autonomy. It differs from coercive power in that B may not realise she has been hindered in achieving her goal.

If a woman decides to enter the workforce she may be met with impedimental power. In the first instance if a woman applies for a job for which she is qualified, but is unsuccessful in securing it. She is given as a reason from her potential employer that her qualifications were not sufficiently high. This could very likely be a case of impedimental power being exercised in a formal situation while the employer in reality did not want to employ a woman. She might not realise that she has been hindered in securing the job. A change in the laws can sometimes reduce the effectiveness of impedimental power.

Legitimate power

The ERA — Equal Rights Amendment (1972) — in the US makes the above example illegal on the grounds that it is discrimination on the basis of sex.[8] The woman in such a case would have the right of appeal which, if successful, would enable her to take up the position. She would first of all have to believe she had been impeded. The employer in this case would have to give way to the decision because of its legitimacy.

Legitimate power (or authority) '... is the right to command and correlatively, the right to be obeyed' (Wolff 1970, p. 4).

The above is an example of a particular type of legitimate power viz. rational authority (to use Weberian terminology). The employer obeys the decision because it has a particular source. Conflict is normally absent even when B disagrees with A's orders, commands, or decision but nevertheless obeys A because of a belief in the legitimacy of the order.

Legitimate power is most common in institutions but it can and does also occur in informal social situations for exactly the same reasons.

Attrahent power

A form of power used almost continually in social relationships, though usually much diluted, is attrahent power. This is power that results from B wanting to be like A or be liked by A. A stronger

---

8 *The ERA has never been ratified, so although in 1976 I thought that discrimination would be illegal, it has provided no protection under law. Discrimination laws in Australia and many other countries on the basis of race and sex have extended the basis for appeals against such discrimination.*

form results when B is devoted to or loves A. This is similar to legitimate power in that B complies with A's wishes just because they are A's wishes, that is because of their source, not because of any official or traditional power vested in A.

On an individual level, which is where the exercise of this form of power is most effective, romantic love affords us an ideal example. If a woman loves a man then she might comply with his wishes just because they are his wishes. She might do things for him that she would not do for others. This may apply in any situation where one person loves another. It is not always a destructive form of power or one that implies conflict.

Persuasive power
Lastly there is persuasive power which de Crespigny divides into two classes:

The first is rational persuasive power which is '... exerted only when the reasons produced in favour of some action are such as would be said to constitute the premises of a (good) argument' (de Crespigny 1970, p. 51).

There is no deception or withholding of information involved in the use of this sort of power, and it is of an advisory nature based on good intentions and reasonable argument.

De Crespigny does not state what he thinks would constitute the second non-rational persuasive power except negatively by saying that it would be rational if the reasons were good. Thus it seems that non-rational power could be based on misinformation, deliberate deception, emotive arguments or bad reasoning. Sales and advertising techniques and the tricks used by con men and fraudsters could be included.[9]

Rational persuasive power implies absence of conflict and allows liberty in the 'negative' sense for B, but is consistent with B's autonomy if choices are available. However, non-rational persuasion is incompatible with B's autonomy.

> Exercises of persuasive power ... are consonant with B's liberty in the 'negative sense since he (*sic*) is not being prevented by others from acting as he (*sic*) pleases. However, some modes of non-rational persuasion are incompatible with the autonomy of a man (*sic*) and are therefore an infringement of his (*sic*) freedom, understood as rational self mastery (de Crespigny 1970, p. 52).

An example of rational persuasion might be advising a woman to use reliable and safe contraceptives if she is going to have sexual intercourse with a man and does not want to become pregnant. Various good reasons may be given for the use of particular forms or combinations of contraception according to her medical history. If, however, she were to become pregnant and was advised to jump from great heights or to have a mustard bath — in order to induce a miscarriage — that would constitute non-rational persuasion.

So far as these seven forms of power are concerned I would argue that women have access to, and thus exercise, only limited forms of power. The forms to which women have access most readily are attrahent and persuasive power. But even within

---

9   *The forces of social media would count in the contemporary world as would easy access to pornography and gambling sites on the Internet.*

these two forms the possibility of, and thus effectiveness of, exercising them is limited.

For instance, in the case of attrahent power this is available to women who have 'developed their personalities'. They are able to 'charm' others, and this means they may gain greater access to other forms of power. However, a man who has access to attrahent power already has access to more and more effective forms of power. A woman relating to such a man will almost always gain prestige, whereas a man relating to a woman with access to attrahent power (and it applies to other forms of power to which women have access) will rarely gain in prestige in a comparable way. What is more likely is that he will be said to be a lucky man to have 'caught' such a charming (or whatever) woman. He is credited with having the power in the first place.

Persuasive power is available to women, both of the rational and non-rational kind. Rational persuasive power is enhanced by high education and/or at least the opportunities for it. Many women, though they might not be explicitly denied education, are generally not encouraged in the way in which men are.[10] Within this form of power, women's power is at its most equal, but still more likely less than men's power. One particularly favourable aspect of rational persuasion is that if it is successful it is usually stable because it relies on A changing B's attitudes or motivations towards some action and thus it can have long term

---

10 *Educational opportunities for girls have improved in western countries, but due to poverty, war, patriarchal tradition and sex-role stereotypes, girls still struggle to get access to meaningful education in many countries around the world.*

effects. Furthermore, it is a socially acceptable means of getting one's way because B accepts it (successful persuasion), i.e. the recipient complies willingly. This may account for the way in which women are seen as powerful, e.g. 'behind every great man is a woman' or the powerful mother figure or because of the way in which women have used their powers of persuasion, rational and non-rational. It also accounts for the charge of emotionality and illogicality laid against women who through frustration and lack of access to other forms of power be a last resort to non-rational persuasion. Non-rational persuasion is the form of power to which many people have ready access and it is the least effective of all the forms identified, particularly in comparison with coercive and legitimate power, both of which are readily accessible to most men. These have the most immediate and effective results and one backed by the other is a very strong combination. This is not to deny that some women have access to extensive and/or effective forms of power but even these women are unlikely to be able to utilise them as readily or as effectively as most men.

To take legitimate power as an example, in order for women to have access to it means that they must be in a position of authority. Very few women are in such positions and that denies access to most women. Most women who are in such positions are there only on the proviso that they conform strictly to the roles expected of them. As a result, many women in those positions are subject to coercive, inducive and reactional power and they almost certainly face impedimental power in their bid for the position. That is, the positions that women gain are positions of *lesser* authority.

The vast majority of women are not in positions of authority. This is in contrast to the large numbers of men who are (being male is sometimes its own authority). And, most men exercise power over women. The ranges of forms of power available to men are greater as are the instances of their exercise. This renders unequal relations between men and women highly probable. Such relations are endorsed by the patriarchy. To claim as some writers have (e.g. Held 1973–74) that women and men can, despite the power differentials in society at large, have equality in power in the sexual sphere if men renounce rape (Held 1973–74, p. 176) and secondly that 'people can and sometimes do renounce the use of power in sexual relationships' (Ketchum and Pierce 1975, p. 8) does not mean that there *is* an equality of power. The sex class of men has not collectively renounced rape, an instance of coercive power. So long as the system endorses the continuation of power-based relations which are weighted in favour of men, then even if some men do renounce their use of power as individuals, this does not mean they have given up their access to power. Power cannot be equal in access to, or exercise of, in a society that systematically favours and endorses the activities of one group. As Dair Gillespie concludes:

> The equalitarian marriage as a norm is a myth. Under some conditions women can gain power vis-à-vis their husbands, i.e. working women [and] women with higher educations than their husbands, have more power than housewives or women with lesser or identical educations ... but more power is not equal power. Equal power we do not have. Equal power we will never get so long as the present socioeconomic system remains. (Gillespie 1975, p. 86).

Equal power is not possible in any sense in a society where economic, social and sexual relations are *power-based*. It is anathema to a sexist-, racist-, capitalist-based state to have equality of power, and it is precisely in the male/female, white/black, employer/worker situations that this inequality manifests itself most obviously.

1.2 Oppression

Any situation in which A objectively exploits B or hinders his (*sic*) pursuit of self-affirmation as a responsible person is one of oppression. Such a situation in itself constitutes violence, even when sweetened by false generosity, because it interferes with man's [*sic*] ontological and historical vocation to be more fully human (Freire 1972, p. 34).

Dehumanisation, the antithesis of Freire's 'ontological and historical vocation' for people, is one of the effects of oppression. It dehumanises the oppressed because they are continually seen as being less than human; they are objects for the pleasure or benefit of the oppressors.

Objects are defined according to their users' intentions or to its capacity (if mechanical[11]) to perform certain tasks. Women are capable of, or have the capacity, to reproduce. Thus they differ in one significant respect from men (provided they are fertile). This

---

11 *This also includes digital objects or any other object lacking consciousness.*

difference of capacity has been used by men to exploit women and limit them to this function. Men have defined women's function by her capacity.[12] Thus women here are objects — her function defined, not by herself, but by others. Thus she is an object. As this definition is based on certain sexual differences and women are defined according to male values and men's sexuality, women are treated as sex objects.

Women's sexuality has been largely ignored independent of men's sexuality. The myth of the vaginal orgasm is an instance of this. Penile penetration has been considered necessary for orgasm for women. Women, according to Freudians, have been classed as sexually immature if vaginal intercourse was not seen as the central means to achieve satisfaction.[13]

Women have been seen as objects whose sexuality can be exploited for pleasure or gain by men. The continuation of seeing women as sex objects means that men continue to contribute to the oppression of women and facilitate sexual exploitation of women by men. Exploitation and oppression, though distinct, support each other, i.e. exploitation acts to reinforce oppression; oppression increases the vulnerability of women to exploitation.

Exploitation is a relation in which the exploiter must be a person or group of persons; the exploitees may be persons or non-persons (e.g. the environment). Oppression on the other hand requires that the oppressed be persons while non-persons can be oppressive (e.g. weather).

---

12 Atkinson distinguishes between capacity and function in 'Abortion Paper' Number II in *Amazon Odyssey* (Atkinson 1974, pp. 1–3)

13 See further discussion of this in the section on heterosexuality.

Resulting from this it follows that as an exploiter

> [O]ne could intentionally *use* persons or things for one's own gain (without regard for their interests in the case of persons) and so exploit, without it being true that one set out institutionally to *be* an exploiter (Tormey 1973–74, p. 209; italics in original).

Exploitation results in one person gaining (exploiter) and the other losing (exploitee).

Oppression, on the other hand, can result in the oppressed *being* oppressed despite the fact that they do not *feel* oppressed. (The oppressor may be unaware also even while exploiting the oppressed.) Internalisation of the oppressors' values by the oppressed is a feature of oppressive relations that is not inherent in exploitative relations. Moreover, in an exploitative relation the exploiter gains; in an oppressive relation, the oppressed can sometimes gain in the short term, as may the oppressor, but both lose in the long term.[14] The distinction is thus a distinction in terms of gains in the short term, at least, for the exploiter, i.e. for only one party of the relation; and losses in the long term for both parties in the oppressive relation. In an exploitative relation there is a chance of long-term gain if both parties are not part of an oppressive situation. Or as Tormey puts it:

---

14 *An example of this is the prostitution industry. Pro-prostitution apologists are arguing that they want to end exploitation and therefore the industry should be regulated and legalised. Abolitionists, on the other hand, are arguing that we need to end prostitution in order to abolish sexual oppression, decriminalise women and put the responsibility of acts of prostitution on men. For further reading see Barry 1979; Barry 1995; Jeffreys 1997; Stark and Whisnant 2004; Ekman 2013; Moran 2013; Raymond 2013; Norma and Tankard Reist 2016; Bindel 2017.*

One of the more important differences between exploitation and oppression is the fact that someone may oppress another person without gaining anything from that oppression, whereas exploitation necessarily involves gain. I am not denying that gain is usually the motive for some forms of oppression, especially those which accompany and facilitate exploitation. That gain may be the motive, however, does not imply that someone *must* gain from oppression ... In fact, it has been noted that because oppression prevents persons from functioning fully in the ways they could function if they were not hampered by truncated self-images and lack of self-respect everyone, oppressor and oppressed alike often loses (Tormey 1973–74, p. 209; italics in original).

This ties in with the dehumanising effect of oppression on the oppressor and the oppressed identified by Freire (1972, p. 24).

The oppressed are dehumanised because they are not seen to have needs and interests of their own and thus are not treated as autonomous and responsible beings. However, in this process of dehumanisation, the oppressors also become dehumanised because of the relation between exploitation and oppression, and, as mentioned above, the two perpetuate and reinforce one another. It applies to the other side of the coin. Exploitation is made easier by oppression but not necessarily more successful. 'And the more the oppressors control the oppressed, the more they change them into apparently inanimate "things"' (Freire 1972, p. 35).

This means that the oppressors are thrown into almost continual contact with 'objects' or dehumanised beings which in turn dehumanises them, the oppressors. If the oppressors are also dehumanised, as they are, this works as a further way of dehumanising the oppressed and perpetuating their oppression. It does so through the mechanism of identifying with the oppressor and internalising, in this case, male values, i.e. believing the 'norms' as set out by patriarchy.

Identifying with men means that women themselves become, as is often said, 'their own worst enemies'. What this means is that through internalising male values, women come to value and devalue the same activities and traits as men do. For instance, women's work in the home, the office or the factory are all devalued and are either paid less or not at all. All are necessary work but because certain occupations — such a housewifery, secretarial work, factory work (especially textiles), teaching, nursing, and so on — have mostly been done by women, they have low status. Those occupations which are predominantly male e.g. medicine, dentistry, engineering, management, have high status; even 'low status' male jobs e.g. labouring, driving, mining, farm work, building are frequently better paid than women's jobs. There are no high status women's jobs. Any high status job a woman might hold is a man's job. At most it is not a sex-specific job.

The same applies to certain traits — male traits such as rational, active, unemotional, responsible turn out to be the 'norm' while female traits such as irrational, passive, emotional, irresponsible, sensitive, turn out to be the traits of 'sick' men but 'healthy' women.

Identification and internalisation perpetuate women's view of themselves and, as they are prescriptive, they eventually become descriptive of women's behaviour.

Women internalise the contradictions that are put forward as women's condition. For instance, if women value and devalue the characteristics prescribed, then they finish up devaluing themselves. If logical thinking is characteristically regarded as a male trait and illogical thinking is characteristically regarded as a female trait, and if women accept their prescribed female role, which includes illogical thinking, then to be successfully 'feminine' they must think illogically, or at least pretend to think in this way. Women become successful as women (or more correctly in this context as 'ladies').[15] If, however, women think logically and furthermore show that they do, they are unsuccessful women because they are not fitting the 'feminine' role. Instead they become successful humans (usually read 'men'). Thus women are faced with a paradox that determines their success either as women or as humans. The two are mutually exclusive.[16] So, if a woman desires to fit the 'feminine' role she must opt for illogicality. The internalisation of the prescribed behaviour thus becomes descriptive of the actual behaviour.

---

15 See Lakoff 1975 for a more detailed analysis of the way in which language systematically denies women access to power. *Suzette Haden Elgin took up this challenge in her novel,* Native Tongue *(1984).*

16 *This paradox is at the root of the glacial pace at which rape has been recognised as a violation of human rights. Only when rape occurred on a mass scale in the former Yugoslavia was it possible for this to be recognised at the level of the United Nations Security Council which set up an international was crimes tribunal in May 1993. Such recognition, which came with the UN Resolution 1820 (2008), has not stopped mass rape from occurring. See Stiglmayer (1994) and United Nations Human Rights Office of the High Commission, 'Rape Weapon of War' 2019.* <https://www.ohchr.org/en/newsevents/pages/rapeweaponwar.aspx>

Concomitant with this is the internalisation of the male disapproval of illogicality, to which she is committed if she is to be successfully female. Her femininity is a manifestation of the internalised behaviour and disapproval — hence conflict. If feminine behaviour is not demonstrated, there is disapproval — hence conflict again. Women face a double bind: whichever way they turn there is disapproval.

Due to internalisation of the oppressors' values and ideology, the oppressed are less able to fight against their oppression because

- either they don't realise they are oppressed (i.e. they can be oppressed without feeling oppressed);
- or else, if they see their own oppression, the internalised values of the oppressor class, often self-damning for the oppressed, prevents them from successfully freeing themselves because this immediately puts them into conflict with themselves.

> The oppressed, having internalized the image of the oppressor and adopted his guidelines, are fearful of freedom. Freedom would require them to eject this image and replace it with autonomy and responsibility (Freire 1972, pp. 23–4).[17]

Ti-Grace Atkinson comments on this in relation to power, which she says has always been seen to be the 'answer' for those wanting political change (i.e. to take power). She says:

---

17 Freedom, as here used, can be achieved using strategies such as consciousness raising.

Without questioning this "answer", no fundamental change can occur.

And yet, how few are willing to give up the power relationship. Even the power*less* cling to the ideology, the hope that as long as the *idea* exists they have hope of escaping power*less*ness by achieving *some* way, *some*how, power*ful*ness. Of course, as long as the conceptual framework of "power" itself is valued (especially if valued by the Oppressed) *none* of us has *any* hope (Atkinson 1974, p. xxii; italics and capitals in original).

The powerless cling to the ideology because they believe in the *legitimacy* of it.

When women internalise the oppressors' patriarchal values, they must accept their own inferiority. The oppressors believe in their superiority, and the system set up by them maintains this structure by allowing greater access to power to members of the oppressor group; and endorsing almost all exercises of this power over the oppressed group. The oppressors are therefore much more powerful than the oppressed. If the oppressed identify with other members of the oppressed group, or with members of other oppressed groups, it is admitting their power*less*ness. By identifying with the oppressors then, the oppressed can gain some feeling of power*ful*ness which ameliorates the conditions of their daily lives. Identifying with the oppressor enables the oppressed to be disparaging about members of their own group, and because they are in agreement with the views of the oppressor group they will have reason (legitimacy) in believing in their rightness. This is destructive to the view the oppressed have of themselves. For instance, the charge of illogicality

- if women accept this, it is damaging to their self-esteem;

- if women accept this of other, or most women, but not themselves, then it divides women.

Identification with the oppressor is a result of being oppressed and maintains disunity among the oppressed.

Moreover, because the values held by the oppressed who have accepted (i.e. internalised) their oppression, are the oppressors' values, this leads to alienation from the world structured, organised and run by the oppressors. Alienation leads to what Freire calls 'domesticating' the oppressed. This occurs when one's perception of reality is distorted. If one is not in direct contact with the world and unable to be critical of it, then distortion is highly probable.

Distortions occur when one is estranged from the public world and the longer one is estranged the harder it becomes to see it without distortion. So much of women's existence is tied to the familiar family unit, and so rarely does she go beyond this that the world seems strange and often dangerous. Many women have contact with the world only or primarily through a male intermediary: a father, husband, lover, brother, son or nephew. Distortions are thus generated through fear of the strange.[18]

If, furthermore, there is widespread mystification of economic, political and social mechanisms then distortion is

---

18 The strange is the public realm; the familiar is the private realm.
   Most people in this society are objects ... [the] division between men and women [is] that men deal with the strange directly and women deal with the strange only through their men, but this information, for most women, is closer to being tenth hand than second hand ... Most men relate to the strange through the mediations of their superiors in the male hierarchy (Allegro 1975, p. 75).

even more likely. The role of 'silence' also plays an important role.[19]

The estrangement of women from the public world has meant that women have been deemed to have done little of historical worth, instead they have remained within the familiar realm of the family. This 'silence' about women's past has worked to maintain the silence about women's present, and women's potential. The 'culture of silence', as Freire calls it, is a powerful tool of oppression. For example, women's sexuality was not scientifically investigated until Masters and Johnson.[20] Instead, the myth of vaginal orgasm was promulgated and, as a consequence, many women were [mis]labelled either frigid or sexually immature.

1.3 Domination

When the access to, and exercise of, power is concentrated in the hands of one group in a society then it may be said that that group is in a position of domination, while the other group or groups are in a position of subordination. The group of persons in the dominant position will do everything to maintain a system that

---

19 *I take up this issue in many subsequent publications (Hawthorne 2007b) See also,* The Spinifex Quiz Book *(1993).*

20 *In her book* Anticlimax *(1990/2011) Sheila Jeffreys points out that the research by Masters and Johnson on sex therapy was used to cure men's sexual problems and ensure their dominance (Jeffreys 2011, p. 134).*

favours them; those in the subordinate position, on the other hand, have very little to lose and much to gain by change in the allocation of power, or an elimination of power-based relations altogether, depending of course on the degree of subordination.

> Domination is characterized by an interest in the maintenance of a social structure that conveys authority, whereas the other — that of subjection — involves an interest in changing a social condition that deprives its incumbents of authority. The two interests are in conflict (Dahrendorf 1970, p. 65).

This means that it is in the interest of the subordinate group to change the structures. It does not mean that all members of the subordinate group want changes to occur — because of the psychological effects of domestication, internalisation of the dominant values, identification with the oppressor group, and a belief in the authority of the institutions that maintain the structures.

The dominant group on the other hand has no reason to change the existing structure of relations. It is not in their interests to change these, whereas the maintenance of them is. Men, as members of the dominant group in patriarchy, have greater access to all forms of power, and they are encouraged to exercise this power, or at the very least most instances of its exercise are endorsed. By radically changing the structure of relations, the scope and effectiveness of men's power would be decreased.

A dominant group is one whose members systematically have access to, and exercise of, more forms of power; and moreover that the values held by the dominant group, i.e. those that work in the interest of members of the group, are protected by tradition or law. This gives authority to them in the Weberian sense. Tradition provides reasons for compliance by members of the subordinate group.

If tradition is not sufficient, as it rarely is in modern pluralistic societies, then the dominant group might protect its interests by applying legal sanctions to actions or behaviour that contravene the interests of the dominant group.[21]

These two forms of power are most important in institutions in which behaviour is largely prescribed. Institutions maintain and perpetuate the values of the dominant group and selectively allow access to, and exercise of, power by members of that group.

1.4 Institutions

One definition of an institution cited and used by Ti-Grace Atkinson is

John Rawls's definition of "practice" = any form of activity specified by a system of roles which defines offices, rules, moves, penalties, defences, and so on, and which gives the activity its structure + Weber's definition of "institutional" = organized so as to function in

---

21 *A recent strategy is to make compliance seem cool, hot, sexy, entertaining, such as the increasing power of the pornography industry and its reach across society even into primary schools. See* Getting Real: Challenging the Sexualisation of Girls *(Tankard Reist 2009).*

social, charitable, and educational activities (Atkinson 1974, p. 13, footnote 2).

To put this in a slightly different way, an institution

1. functions to control people's actions, behaviour, in at least one sphere;
2. allocates particular tasks or roles for people within an institution according to their status, credentials etc., and disallows or at least discourages too much flexibility of roles or tasks; most frequently it is hierarchical;
3. the institution has authority over the people in it (or its officers included) and frequently also affects people outside it.

Institutions are an important controlling agent because people in their interactions with institutions are not able to deviate from the prescribed roles too much. Sanctions may be applied if they do, and, as the institutions dictate the rules, then somebody entering an institution does so with the knowledge (tacit at least) that deviations are, in general, not permissible. Compliance is maximised because those giving the orders, prescribing the rules, etc. are placed at the top of the hierarchical ladder, and they also have access to coercive power. Even if a person does not agree with a particular order or rule within an institution, she nevertheless usually complies for one or both of two reasons. Firstly, because she believes in the authority of the order; or secondly, because she knows that coercive power may be exercised if she does not comply. Compliance on these grounds is fairly obvious within the confines of public institutions. For instance, most people most of the time comply with the laws, either because they believe in them, or because they know they could be punished if they did not.

Compliance on these grounds is less obvious but still applicable to persons within institutions that are less visible. For instance, within the institution of heterosexuality most people, most of the time, comply with the roles expected of them according to their sex. They do so because they either believe in its authority (traditional or legal), or because they believe that if they do not comply, then they might be punished or deprived in some way.

Chapter 2
Things Peculiar to Women's Oppression

2.1 Heterosexuality

Heterosexuality fits the criteria, spelled out above, for an institution.

1. It formalises the relations between women and men and consequently controls and limits the possible relations between people in at least the sexual sphere.

2. Particular tasks and roles are allocated to women and men within the institution. These differ according to the sex of the person. It is not generally acceptable for women to initiate sexual activity, whereas men are expected to. This preserves the respective subordinate/dominant positions of women and men. Flexibility within heterosexual relations is minimised.

3. Heterosexuality has authority over the people in it, including men, and it also affects people who are not involved in heterosexual relations because it is the acceptable model of relating.

Institutions give authority to oppression and the pervading ideology supplies the reasons for the oppression. Furthermore, it provides the reasons for oppression and the reasons for the authority given to the institution. Of the three forms of authority supplied by Weber's analysis, the relevant two here are traditional authority and legal authority.

Authority is

> ... "traditional" if legitimacy is claimed for it and believed in on the basis of the sanctity of the order, and the attendant powers of control as they have been handed down from the past, "have always existed" (Weber in Olsen 1970, p. 36).

Heterosexuality is believed to be the natural form of sexuality. In the past, it has frequently resulted in children. Children were important for survival so heterosexuality framed this way can be seen as a survival tool of the past. This is no longer true, and with over-population it may be contrary to our own and other species survival.[22]

The 'naturalness' of heterosexuality as claimed and supported by traditional authority is reinforced by the commands of legal authority. Legal authority rests on rational grounds that is '... on a belief in the legality of patterns of normative rules and the right of those elevated to authority under such rules to issue commands' (Weber in Olsen 1970, p. 37).

Scientific data has been appealed to in order to support the claims of legislators who endorse legislation that outlaws other forms of sexual behaviour. Scientific research that

---

22 *I now think this is a poor argument. The problem is not over-population, but over-consumption especially by the richer classes and those in countries where consumption is encouraged. See my book* Wild Politics: Feminism, Globalisation and Bio/diversity *(2002).*

'proves' the naturalness of heterosexuality and concomitantly the 'unnaturalness' of any other sexual activity has been presented. This data is mostly gained by the study of animal behaviour, particularly primates. However, recently different studies have gained evidence to support the opposite thesis, i.e. that heterosexual behaviour is not the only sexual behaviour engaged in by animals. This shift in evidence creates doubt in peoples' heads about so-called objectivity of scientific research, particularly research that affects the authority of patriarchy.

Aside from this, whatever the evidence shows, such extrapolations from studies of animals to claims about human behaviour are methodologically problematic.

Arguments that support heterosexuality based on appeals of naturalness are also problematic. Firstly, there has to be a decision made about what actually constitutes natural behaviour; and secondly, the attachment of the label 'natural' is assumed to make it good, or right, or better. This is a spurious claim. There is no necessary link between natural and good, or unnatural and bad.

To take the second point first, although the Vatican in

... *Humanae Vitae* assumes that it is sufficient to point out that artificial means of birth control interrupt the natural order of things ... Apparently what the "natural order" means in this case is that which will happen if untouched by human invention [or intervention]. This definition however, yields absurd consequences if we try to use it as a prescription. If 'natural order' is a good thing, and we must assume it is because we are told not to interrupt it, why isn't shaving a moral issue? Clearly, it is natural for hair to grow on a man's face, and shaving introduces an artificial means to disrupt the natural order of things (Pierce 1971, pp. 243–4).

And, as Pierce points out, there are two incompatible and distinct notions of 'natural' with regard to human nature.

1. That which is based on commonality of human and animal characteristics;
2. That which distinguishes humans from animals (Pierce 1971, p. 244).

As our notions of what constitutes 'natural' are confused and thus problematic, to appeal to that argument is not likely to clarify anything we might want to say. I will not pursue the 'natural' argument any further because it is a red herring.

I have shown above how heterosexuality fits the criteria for institutions. Like the family it is supported by other institutions that give it authority in this society.[23]

Heterosexuality is supported by the myth of the vaginal orgasm[24] which, it is claimed, if a woman is mature sexually she will experience. Just as mature women, i.e. feminine women, will marry and in so doing support the institution of the family.

---

23 *For a recent discussion of heterosexuality as an institution, see Hawthorne, 2007a. See also Rowland and Klein (1996) and Rowland (1996).*

24 *Discussion of vaginal orgasm has disappeared from public discourse. Indeed, the possibility of women enjoying sexual intimacy has shifted to the back burner and has been replaced by what men want through the increasingly available pornography, especially gonzo porn. See Tankard Reist and Bray (2011); Dines (2010). Sheila Jeffreys writes about orgasm in Chapter 6 of* Anticlimax *(1990/2011).*

Marriage and the family have been questioned fairly extensively in recent years, and so are under threat as institutions.[25] The institution of heterosexuality on the other hand has been challenged by only a few feminist radicals.

Vaginal orgasm supports heterosexual intercourse by

1. Supporting the view that penetration of the vagina by the penis is the only acceptable mode of sexual intercourse; and that it is the most enjoyable mode for both the woman and the man. This claim is questionable for both parties. So far as the woman is concerned unless the clitoris is stimulated in some way, orgasm will not occur. The stimulation may involve other areas such as the labia minora and the vestibule of the vagina, but the clitoris is the centre of orgasm.

> The head of the clitoris is ... composed of erectile tissue and it possesses a very sensitive epithelium of surface covering, supplied with special nerve endings called genital corpuscles, which are peculiarly adapted for sensory stimulation that under proper mental conditions terminates in the sexual orgasm. No other part of the female generative tract has such corpuscles (Kelly cited in Koedt 1973, p. 202).

---

25 *Critiques of the family have also disappeared as the queer generation has opted to fight for same-sex marriage instead. The problem with this is that it confuses, in a postmodern kind of way, heterosexuality and marriage. Critiquing marriage, which remains an oppressive institution, is now seen as a reactionary move. The radical critiques of marriage allowed heterosexual feminists to resist the marriage institution. Since 2001, when the Netherlands legalised gay marriage, many other countries have followed suit. In spite of this, marriage is not a freeing institution, rather lesbians and gay men have married sometimes because of other discriminatory laws on tax or health care, and getting married provides access to these government services. Of course, there are many who crave acceptance by family and community.*

Vaginal orgasm, that is orgasm originating in the vagina is in fact physiologically impossible as the vagina does not possess genital corpuscles that are necessary in causing orgasm. In fact the inside of the vagina has a high degree of insensitivity.

The interior of the vagina is

> ... like nearly all other internal body structures, poorly supplied with end organs of touch. The internal endodermal origin of the lining of the vagina makes it similar in this respect to the rectum and other parts of the digestive tract (Kinsey cited in Koedt 1973, p. 202).

2. Contributing to women's invisibility in a way that is very different from the invisibility of other oppressed groups. For women to be 'sexually mature' they must relate to a man, and if women are deemed to have exclusively vaginal orgasms then men are deemed necessary in order for women to gain sexual pleasure. This means that women's sexuality is associated with men's sexuality. Vaginal orgasm perpetuates the myth that women cannot have sexual lives independent of men. Moreover, it contributes to women's identification with men and in this way contributes to women's invisibility.

3. Men fear women engaging in sexual activity with women. And men such as Freud have perpetuated the myth that the vagina is the only or even the primary source of the vaginal orgasm by either emphasising the importance of vaginal orgasm and vaginas and/or by ignoring the clitoris, and/or denying the existence of clitoral orgasms, and/or associating clitoral orgasm with abnormality and/or immaturity.

4. Emphasising the importance of vaginal orgasm emphasises the importance of the penis and of penetration. Heterosexual relations are thus also emphasised because the penis is seen as necessary for the woman's sexual pleasure, and the vagina is seen as important but not necessary for men's pleasure. If women believe the myth, they are unlikely to think they can gain full sexual pleasure by masturbating as clitoral orgasms are not as satisfying (according to the myth). Sexual intercourse with men then will be seen as the primary source of their pleasure. By contrast, emphasising the importance of clitoral orgasm reverses the situation. Men are thus "sexually expendable" (Koedt 1973, p. 205). The function of the penis for the woman is reduced to its reproductive function.

5. Contributing to men's control over women. If a woman thinks orgasm only occurs through heterosexual intercourse and if birth control methods are unavailable or unreliable — and abortion illegal — then women are less likely to partake in heterosexual relations (for fear of pregnancy) and further are less likely to conceive of satisfactory sexual relations with women (the 'how-do-they-do-it?' syndrome).

6. The patriarchal insistence that the vagina is the only source of orgasm supports the institution of heterosexuality. Tradition and the widespread diffusion of misinformation (e.g. Freud's remarks about women's sexuality) have given the notion of vaginal orgasm authority. By exposing the myth, heterosexuality becomes just one sexual decision among many, and is not the norm against which other decisions are measured. This can lead to an eventual diminution and/or

eradication of feelings of guilt experienced by women who do not experience orgasm during heterosexual intercourse thus making the term 'frigid' as now used, meaningless.

By means of the largely traditional view that heterosexuality is natural, and the only-recently exploded myth of vaginal orgasm, heterosexuality has been inevitable for women.[26] Not so much so for men since masturbation and homosexuality have not been as systematically ignored for men as they have been for women. Moreover, marriage and motherhood were and still do play an important part in female conditioning. These contribute to the maintenance of heterosexuality as an institution. Marriage is the legal formalising of heterosexual relations and within it women's roles and tasks are well defined. As stated in the conventional marriage ceremony: she is wife; he is man. Her identity depends largely on his (including the naming convention: Mrs Jim Brown). A man's identity and future is attached to himself. He is only considered 'deficient' if he fails in the public realm; she, however, is deficient if she is not associated with a man.

> The overall objective of female conditioning is to make women perceive themselves and their lives through male eyes and so to secure their unquestioning acceptance of a male-defined and male-derived existence. The overall objective of male conditioning is to make men perceive themselves and their lives through their own eyes and so prepare themselves for an existence in and on

---

26 *In 1981, Onlywomen Press in London published Adrienne Rich's ground-breaking essay,* Compulsory Heterosexuality and Lesbian Existence *as a pamphlet. It had been published in the USA in the journal,* Signs, *a year earlier. I read the pamphlet.*

their own terms. The combined effect of both ways of conditioning is, therefore, the perpetuation of a power relationship between the sexes. The fact that both sexes are exposed to straight conditioning does not prevent the concept of heterosexuality from being linked — in male and female conditioning respectively — to opposite things that have opposite meanings. In male conditioning, male heterosexuality is linked to the male prerogative of a human identity; in female conditioning, female heterosexuality is linked to the denial of that same identity (The Purple September Staff 1975, p. 81).

That is, man equals human; woman does not. 'Man' is used as a generic term to encompass both men and women — i.e. all humans. 'Woman' is sex specific and not synonymous with 'human'.[27]

So heterosexuality acquires a normative status in marriage and its various forms within the patriarchy, and it is this status that has to be assessed. It

... forces women to limit themselves sexually and emotionally to relationships with members of the caste that oppresses them while denying them the possibility of establishing meaningful relationships with other women (The Purple September Staff 1975, p. 83).

This is not to say that there can be no heterosexual relations that satisfy those in them, but if they are satisfying then it is because

---

27 See earlier discussion on internalisation and 'illogicality', section 1.2.
   This distinction between man as human and woman as not has made it difficult for women's human rights to be recognised as 'human' rights. See MacKinnon, 2007; it continues to make it difficult for lesbian human rights to be recognised, see Hawthorne, 2009.

the people involved in them do not act in accordance with the roles and rules of heterosexuality as an institution.

However, given the accessibility differentials of men and women to forms of power — and thus the option of exercising it or not — such relationships are likely to be few in number.

Consider a hypothetical relationship between a man (M) and a woman (W) both of whom want to eliminate the power basis of their relationship. If M gives up his exercise of power it does not follow that he has given up his access to power. If it is a mutual relationship and W gives up her exercise of power, this does largely result in W giving up her access to power. By mutual, I mean that both attempt to give up their exercise of power. W giving up her exercise of power renders her even more powerless than previously. Whereas for M it does not follow that he has given up his access to power even though he has not exercised it. In a patriarchal society power is accessible to all men, even if not all men exercise this option. This option is not open to all women. Thus the above mutual situation between M and W is once more inequitable.

> ... a mutual renunciation of the use of power is vastly unequal [it] is merely an armed truce and may give the weaker party an illusion of power rather than equality of power (Ketchum and Pierce 1975, p. 10).

For instance, in the above case where both M and W give up their use or exercise of power, W might not realise that M has access to legitimate power. Because we live in a patriarchy and M is a member of the dominant group he has the option of changing his mind.

> As long as the structure of society remains the same, as long as categorical discrimination against women is carried out, there is relatively little chance for one woman to gain autonomy, *regardless* of how much good will there is on the part of the husband (Gillespie 1975, p. 86).

M always has the option, and in this society, the prerogative to *change his mind* (e.g. in rape). Furthermore advantages (e.g. job discrimination where a woman has to surpass male applicants) still accrue to him. M

> ... can no more effectively relinquish the power due to him in a sexist society than a white liberal can relinquish his over Blacks. No matter how sincere the white male is, sexism and racism will operate to his advantage with or without his consent and even the advantages that he is in a position to refuse are waiting for him if he changes his mind (Ketchum and Pierce 1975, p. 11).

Men in a patriarchy are advantaged or privileged in ways that women are not. This advantage offers inducements to women to associate with men because, by doing so, the women can derive some prestige. The prestige gained by associating with a man is necessarily diluted because the prestige gained is mostly a result of something a closely associated man has achieved. A person can have prestige though they may have little access of power.[28]

For example, a woman married to a man with a high income may have prestige with little access to power. In fact, if she is not working and she is economically dependent on her husband and living in the suburbs, then chances are that she will lose access

---

28 *Andrea Dworkin's book,* Right Wing Women (1983) *explicates the process of 'domestication' that women undergo.*

to power. This is because of the large economic differential between the two; and by being suburbanised she is more likely to be cut off from close associates such as friends and family.[29]

The chances of most women stepping outside the institution of heterosexuality are still fairly low. Though the inducements of heterosexuality may not be as great as they appear to be, the possible hardships that could ensue from choosing relationships with women prevent women from refusing to conform to heterosexual norms. In the long term, the latter can enable women to build up a life independent of the models provided. But the heterosexual mode of relating will not be easily budged. By this I mean not the act of heterosexual intercourse but those things that make heterosexual relations unequal. This includes the power differentials between men and women; other institutions within patriarchy which support such relations; the ideology which gives reasons for the existence of such institutions.

> The ideology of heterosexuality ... is the whole set of assumptions and beliefs which maintains the ideological power of men over women. It is the basic framework which determines a woman's life from the earliest moments she learns to perceive the world. It tells her what is natural that she be and do.
>
> Heterosexual hegemony insures that people think it natural that male and female form a life long sexual/reproductive unit ... [It insures] that people's sexuality [is not] totally divorced from reproduction ... Heterosexual hegemony insures that people can't even perceive that there could be other possibilities (Small 1975, p. 58).

---

29 See Gillespie (1975) for further details on this.

Alternatives are beginning to be devised,[30] however, at present the main mode of relating is heterosexuality. Two very important supports of the institution, rape and love will be discussed before I say anything more about alternative modes of relating.

2.2 Rape

Rape is a manifestation of coercive power by men over women (primarily).[31] It is an act which exploits the power differentials between men and women. It is a form of coercive power to which women have no access (other than with children); all men on the other hand have access to it (discounting those with physical handicaps) although not all men exercise this option.[32] As pointed out previously

---

30 See discussion in Chapter 3, pp. 68–74. *In the period following 1976, there were numerous actions carried out by women e.g. the women's lands in Australia and many similar communities in countries around the world. Women's organisations in politics, science and arts flourished for a few years, until the backlash which began in the late 1980s.*

31 It could be argued that rape in a homosexual context is still a heterosexual crime because the man being raped is generally seen as effeminate, that is, like a woman. He has stepped outside the prescribed personal relations. See Kate Millett on Genet in *Sexual Politics* (1972).

32 *Susan Brownmiller (1976) made this point in* Against Our Will. *Her argument is frequently misread as 'all men are rapists' instead of rape is 'a conscious process of intimidation by which all men keep all women in a state of fear.' (Brownmiller 1976, p. 15). The astute reader might be wondering why I did not cite Brownmiller in my thesis? While the book was published in the US*

... the important thing is not that there are men who do not exercise the option they have. The important thing is that the option exists whether or not it is exercised (The Purple September Staff 1975, p. 83).

Thus not all men need to actually rape a woman, just as not all women need to have been raped, for it to be an act which maintains the institution of heterosexuality. That is, it maintains the power differentials between men and women.[33]

Rape preserves heterosexual hegemony by actually, or potentially, threatening women who do not measure up to the prescribed standards of behaviour for women.[34] It is one of the deprivations — or threats of deprivation — which face all women. It supports the inducements of heterosexuality. Women are led to believe, by the 'myth of rape', that they will be largely free from the threat of its exercise if they remain within prescribed bounds. The 'myth of rape' is that only women who are promiscuous, who walk the streets alone (that is without a man) at night are likely to be raped and that they will be raped by a man who is a stranger. In this context it can be seen as punishment inflicted on those who do not abide by the behaviour expected of women

---

in 1975, Penguin in the UK only published it in 1976. I bought my copy in August 1977 (inscribed on the inside cover).

33 *In the period after the end of slavery in the USA, lynching played a similar role. For further reading on this see my 2011 essay 'Capital and the Crimes of Pornographers'.*

34 *Many decades after writing this I wrote a poem, 'How do you protect yourself from rape?'. First published in English and Spanish online and later in books. Hawthorne (2016; 2017). This and other writings by me reflect my own experiences.*

in patriarchy. A large proportion of rapes take place indoors and are committed by men who have had some prior contact with the woman. The myth, however, continues to be promulgated by the media and other sources and in doing so many women react to this belief (reactional power) and are alert to the purported dangers of going out alone to deserted places or of being in the streets either during the day or night. Because of this apprehension or fear women are deprived of their autonomy and freedom of movement.[35] As a result, women frequently turn to another man for protection.

Historically, rape was originally a crime against property — the woman was considered the property of the man. This is tacitly still the case in the sense that a woman who has a monogamous association with one man has a better chance of a successful prosecution of the rapist, providing he can be found and identified.[36] If this is not the case, then a woman's chances of successful prosecution are increased if the victim

---

35 *Thirty-five years after writing this the rape cases that get the most media attention are those that fit the 'myth of rape.' Jill Meagher, raped and killed in Melbourne in 2012 and Eurydice Dixon, raped and murdered in 2018; and Jyoti Singh Pandey gang raped in Delhi, who died as a result of the injuries inflicted on her in 2012. These three rapes have received massive media attention, demonstrations, vigils and commentary. Many more rapes have happened invisibly in women's homes by men known to them.*

36 *The above cases are also unusual because in all three instances the perpetrator(s) could be identified. In the crimes against Jill Meagher and Eurydice Dixon, video identification provided evidence; in Jyoti Singh Pandey's case her boyfriend witnessed the rape (and was also violated). Most rape prosecutions fail because electronic or human witnesses are not available.*

has obvious, that is visible signs of violence. Moreover, a woman cannot have her husband prosecuted for rape because he is still her property.[37]

These matters are largely empirical and the purpose of their explication is that they afford evidence for the position I am taking.

If there were readily accessible alternatives to the institution of heterosexuality, and if the foundations were challenged, then the chances of decreasing and eventually eliminating the sexual exploitation and oppression of women would be increased.

Rape provides a clear instance of a power-based relation which manifests itself in the sexual sphere. Rape works to increase and substantiate women's feelings of powerlessness.

2.3 Romantic Love

If power were not unequal then love would be possible between the sexes. In a patriarchy, love becomes an instance of attrahent power. By definition, in a patriarchy, inequality between men and women is institutionalised. Only if the persons involved in a relationship step outside the prescribed roles, can the relation be mutual. This requires that the systematic differences in power

---

37 *In 1976 this was the case. The law was changed in New South Wales, Australia in 1981 but was not a law in all states until 1992. <http://en.wikipedia.org/ wiki/Marital_rape>*

be changed. Mutuality is determined by the relative differentials of access to, and exercise of, power within the relationship.

If the differentials are great and systematically weighted in favour of one party — but the feelings of love are mutual — then chances are high that it is an oppressive situation. In the case of men and women most men have access to more power and more forms of power than most women (see Chapter 1.1 pp. 17–30).

This means that the relationship is unlikely to be mutual. Romantic love is mostly love that is not mutual. Romantic love is thus likely to be oppressive. Romantic love is celebrated by the media which reinforces the oppression of women. It exploits the difference in power held by men and women. To reiterate: most men have more power than most women. One way in which women can gain prestige and psychological encouragement within the patriarchal system is by knowing that a man — a member of the dominant group — approves of her and says he loves her. Some women may superficially benefit psychologically from this knowledge, but in the long term most women become psychologically dependent, either on that man or on the approval of other men in the society.

Men express this 'approval' when they whistle at women in the street; women are meant to take it as a compliment on their appearance — what this really amounts to is exploitation and commodification of women via their sexuality. That is, women are seen as sex objects.

In order to gain such approval, women must spend a disproportionate amount of their time on things such as appearance, cultivation of a 'personality' (bubbly, likeable, sexy) and so on. This keeps women 'domesticated' and turned inward. As a result, their attention is diverted away from affairs of the world. This includes diverting a woman's attention away from her own oppression.

Moreover, love plays a more central role in the lives of women than it does in the lives of men. Byron's claim that 'Man's love is of man's life, a thing apart, 'Tis woman's whole existence' condenses suitably the differing importance of romantic love in women's and men's lives and alludes to the power differentials created by the differing importance of love for women and men.

Firestone (1972, p. 126) and Atkinson (1974, p. 43) have both argued that love is the 'pivot' of women's oppression and that reactions to analyses of love which threaten its existence are 'clues to the political significance of love' (Firestone 1972, p. 121).

Atkinson is somewhat more critical than Firestone about whether love even exists. Firestone's main argument is that love

> ... becomes complicated, corrupted, or obstructed by *an unequal balance of power* ... love demands a mutual vulnerability or it turns destructive: the destructive effects of love occur only in a context of inequality. But because sexual inequality has remained a constant — however its *degree* may have varied — the corruption 'romantic' love became characteristic of love *between* the sexes (Firestone 1972, p. 124; my emphasis).

Virginia Held suggests that couples should engage in 'experiments in love' as a strategy because this would quicken the actualisation of love *between* men and women. And though she admits these experiments may be costly to women, attempting and failing is better than not attempting at all. However, this puts the onus back on women to make life liveable for men. Held argues that

> [A] relation of mutuality is quite different from a relation of power where two persons, as entities possessing power, stand in some factual relation to one another, as when we can empirically describe that one person has greater power than another. A relation of mutual concern and respect is also different, although both are conscious, social relations, from a more mutual recognition by each person of the factual relation of power in which they stand, even when it is one of equal power. Equality is in general a precondition for a relation of mutual concern between man and woman, but we do not necessarily have such a relation with any equal, nor is it in *all* cases absent when power is unequal.
>
> By the relation of mutual concern and respect in its distinctive sense we mean a relation in which neither person uses the other, neither sees the other primarily as a means to satisfaction of his or her own self interest. The relation is genuinely mutual; it is only achievable together and consciously (Held 1973–74, p. 172, emphasis in the original).

Held states that 'equality is a ... precondition for a relation of mutual concern' (Held 1973–74, p. 172). Particular instances of coercive power used by men in oppressing women must cease. To do this requires the de-institutionalisation of heterosexuality, that is, *most* men must stop *using* the power to which they have access in patriarchy, because patriarchy endorses most of these occurrences.

Even if it could be argued that mutuality is possible without equality in all cases, i.e. that the vast majority of men retain their power — and systematically exercise it — is sufficient to show that mutual relations are highly improbable between men and women.

To then suggest that women should engage in 'experiments in love' (Held 1973-74, p. 172) as a strategy does not seem very good advice.

Moreover, if it is to women that this suggestion is directed, then a contradiction immediately arises: that it is putting the onus on women to love men (members of the dominant group) increases the likelihood of the continuation of women identifying with men — of wanting men's approval — and thereby of maintaining the institution of heterosexuality.

Furthermore, if it is 'only achievable together' (Held 1973-74, p. 172) the onus of loving should not be on women. It is inconsistent with Held's position on mutual relations.

It is also interesting to note that although Held advocates loving men as a strategy, she nevertheless recognises that "... women will have to accept a kind of schizophrenic existence" (Held 1973-74, p. 176) so as to fight and love the oppressor at the same time. She fails to see that by questioning romantic love between men and women, and by considering other modes of relating, this 'schizophrenic existence' could be avoided.

By loving men, women are placed in a highly vulnerable position which makes them more easily exploitable. Endorsing the present mode of relating — by partaking in loving within the institution of heterosexuality — women's present position of oppression is reinforced.

Held's mutual 'experiments in love' are logically impossible if Atkinson's definition of love is accepted. She distinguishes between 'friendship' and 'love'.

> 'Friendship' is a rational relationship which requires the participation of two parties to the mutual satisfaction of both parties. 'Love' can only be felt by one party; it is unilateral by nature, and, combined with its relational character, it is thus rendered contradictory and irrational (Atkinson 1974, p. 44).

I part with Ti-Grace Atkinson here as I do think that love is possible between two people one or other of who is not systematically advantaged. If one or the other is not systematically advantaged or disadvantaged then I also think that it can be mutual and it may thus be properly called 'love'.

I agree that friendships are more usually mutual in our society. This is so because friends see themselves as equals (usually) and, as Held points out, inequality does not prevent mutuality in all cases.[38] What she fails to see is that systematic inequality — or institutionalised inequality — does. Take for example a relation between a parent and child: a mutual relation between the two is not only unlikely, it would also be dangerous to the wellbeing of the child. Only when the child gains the means by which she or he may increase her or his access to power — in so doing decreasing the power differential — can the relation begin to be mutual (i.e. through the attainment of adulthood).

A child does not have a 'choice' or the power to 'make decisions' so the relationship cannot be mutual on Held's

---

38 For *a fine philosophical discussion of friendship from a radical feminist point of view see Janice G. Raymond's* A Passion for Friends *(1986; 2002).*

criteria that 'it is only achievable together and consciously' (Held 1973–74, p. 172) by both parties (I take 'consciously' to mean that a conscious decision has been made). Although not mutual by Held's definition, a parent–child relationship built on care should be mutually beneficial.

If, as I have argued above, identification with the oppressor ameliorates the feelings of powerlessness of the oppressed, than by loving the oppressor — the love accepted — lessens the feelings of powerlessness. If the oppressed are loved this probably makes them feel less powerless. Romantic love between women and men perpetuates women's conditions of oppression by diverting their attention from other women's condition and thus from her own oppression. Romantic love is a source of oppression that is not easily located because of the myths that surround it, but that does not make it any less insidious. If anything, it should make us more wary of entering into 'experiments in love' that do not have a high chance of mutuality.

To conclude, when one party is systematically advantaged — as men are in a patriarchy — then I think the chances of mutuality are so low as to be almost exclusive. As a consequence, in patriarchy romantic love is one of the major supports of the institution of heterosexuality.

Chapter 3
Strategies

3.1 Separatism

I propose separatism as a viable strategy for women's liberation.
There is an important distinction that I must make before
defending separatism, and that is between separatism and
segregation. As Lucia Valeska writes:

> The chief difference between the two is how they are used, by whom
> and for what purposes. Segregation is used by the economically
> dominant group as a means of social control, i.e. to maintain and
> perpetuate a given economic, political and social stratification
> system. Whereas separatism is used by the economically
> disadvantaged in order to radically alter existing political, social
> and economic arrangements (Valeska 1975, p. 6).

Segregation is an instance of coercive power, a manifestation
of domination. Separatism is a means of resisting oppression,
a withdrawal of support or action, and potentially a strategy for
liberation. Both are powerful political devices. The distinction
depends on who is initiating the separation and for what purpose.
For example, in South Africa, segregation is used by whites to
keep blacks powerless; if those same blacks have organisational

meetings (virtually impossible under Apartheid in South Africa[39]) and keep whites out, that is separatism. The difference here is between involuntary separation by the oppressed (segregation) and voluntary separation by the oppressed (separatism).

As Valeska states:

> It is differential treatment (legal and illegal) that created the situation and it will, of necessity, be differential treatment that gets us out of it (Valeska 1975, p. 6).

Moreover, feminism is intrinsically separatist, at least minimally, because men are not permitted into consciousness-raising groups, action groups, meetings and most women's centres.[40]

The justifications for these exclusions are usually based on claims that women will be inhibited by or intimidated by men. But the real importance of women working together without men is not confidence or self-esteem but rather that women can affirm their political accord not connected to any male, i.e. women can become separate beings.[41] By doing so women's feelings of fragmentation and alienation can be reduced and

---

39 *From 1948–1994 under the National Party, Apartheid made it legal to discriminate against black people. Everything was segregated e.g. medical services, schools, outdoor venues such as beaches and sporting facilities. Anti-Apartheid politics was a strong force in 1976.*

40 *As noted in the Preface the question of whether women can justify having separate women's spaces has come to the fore again in 2019. As Ti-Grace Atkinson wrote in 1974, 'The paranoia of one's enemy is, frequently, both instructive and inspirational' (Atkinson 1974, p. 132).*

41 *In Marxist terms, it is the equivalent of unalienated labour, the achievement of a complete self, separate from dependence on the employer (in Marxist politics) or on a man or male approval (in feminist politics).*

eventually eliminated. And I believe that the greater proportion of time and/or energy spent working with and for women, the more likely these results will be.

Separatism is wide ranging in degree.

Separatism is an action, event or organisation that enables women to participate separately *for political reasons*. The last part is extremely important for without it tea parties and ladies' auxiliaries would be included which are unlikely to play a role in the liberation of women. Moreover, those situations (tea parties, etc.) are unlikely to lead women changing their consciousness or lead to action which changes social structures.

Here are some of the manifestations of separatism varying in degree:

1. Valuing dialogue with other women e.g. in consciousness-raising groups, study groups, or political action groups.
2. Engaging in political or social action with other women, e.g. abortion action groups, rape crisis groups, newsletter collectives.
3. Partaking in social gatherings in which only women participate, e.g. women's dances. (Remember how women's dances challenged ideas about what it was to have a good time — and that it was possible to do so without men around.)
4. Working in an environment which is run for and by women, e.g. women's health centres, women's publishing, unemployment centres for young women.[42]

---

42 *With changing demographics, there is a need, in 2019, for unemployment centres for old women (50 plus age).*

5. Becoming women-identified, giving emotional support to women, and involving oneself in sexual relations with women (and moreover, refusing to support men in any of the above ways), e.g. lesbian relationships or celibacy.

6. Participating in groups with other women that are concerned with creativity, e.g. theatre groups, writing workshops, art exhibitions, music groups.

7. Living in an all-women environment and having no contact with men. This is usually understood to be the standard separatist position, but is only possible for a limited number of women. Those for whom it is most feasible are women who live in all-women communities in the country. Many urban women limit their contact with men sufficiently to live a strongly separatist lifestyle. While only a few women will live this way, it is important to endorse as a strategy. It has inspirational value and is visible proof that women do not need men for social, financial and physical support.

8. Lesbian separatists might choose to not have contact with heterosexual women in one or more of the above areas.

The forms of separatism listed above need not occur in this order. It is not a hierarchical list whereby one measures one's feminist commitment. It is important to recognise that separatism is a *strategy* engaged in by every feminist. It is a fundamental element of all feminist philosophy.

Separatism has come in for a lot of criticism both from within and without the women's liberation movement. I believe it can withstand the criticisms that have been put forward and that it offers women a powerful political strategy (Hawthorne 1990).[43]

---

43 *The quotation was not in the original thesis, but was included in the 1990 version.*

3.2 Lesbian Feminism

While separatism is the overall strategy, lesbian feminism is one part of that strategy. And while it is a small number of women who engage in it, the political output of these women is significant. It must be noted that lesbians and heterosexual women work together to achieve feminist goals. I have already given an account of the basis of the institution of heterosexuality. It is the major way by which men, members of the dominant group, have oppressed women. Lesbian feminism extends the analysis of women as an oppressed group — and thus a political group — to an analysis of sexuality as it has been used to oppress women in the form of heterosexism; but it is also applicable to other forms of sexual oppression that take heterosexuality as their model.[44]

Such an analysis is important if an oppressed group is to overcome its oppression. That is, the oppressed must first of all locate the way(s) by which they are oppressed and work together to break down the structures that support that oppression and the structures which they support.[45]

Feminist analyses recognise that the relations between men and women are power based and oppressive to women. Here I am highlighting the significance of heterosexuality in relation

---

44 *The growth of SM practice by lesbians in the late 1980s bothered me and I have written extensively about violence. See Hawthorne, 1992.*

45 The myth of vaginal orgasm supports heterosexuality; heterosexuality supports the patriarchy; patriarchy supports the myth of vaginal orgasm.

to the feminist critique of marriage, the family, motherhood, housewifery duties and supportive jobs that support the claims of oppression. Heterosexuality underlies all of the ways that patriarchy maintains women's oppression: its consequences are the major factors contributing to women's limited access to, and exercise of, power.

Atkinson has pointed out that lesbian feminism is essential for a successful change in the nature of power relations in patriarchal society (Atkinson 1974, pp. 131–134). The reason that lesbian feminism is so important is because it lies outside the institution of heterosexuality. That is, it offers women an opportunity to go beyond the structures of 'patriarchal sexuality'. By this I mean any sexual relation where those involved uphold roles and power differentials; the power being systematically accessible to, or exercised by, one party. This can apply to non-heterosexual relations where one party is dominant.[46] The 'classic' heterosexual relation is the model for 'patriarchal sexual relations'. By criticising this model, the lesbian feminist analysis challenges power-based relations and thus their validity as models for relating.

I suggest lesbian feminism as a strategy because as I have argued earlier, relations between women who are feminists are less likely to be unequal in power than relation between men

---

46 *The political contradictions of sado-masochism, BDSM and other dominant-submissive relations continue to pose challenges for contemporary feminists and lesbians. I have written at length elsewhere about these issues. See Hawthorne, 2011.*

and women.[47] Most women have access to — and less exercise of — less power and less effective power. Unless one of the women involved systematically has more power than the other, then the power differential will be less. Moreover, no women within the patriarchy have immediate access to legitimate power in the way that all men do and which establishes the power differential from the start. Lesbian feminist relations are even less likely to be unequal in power if the heterosexual model of relating is rejected on the grounds that it is oppressive.

Lesbian feminism promotes relations between women.[48] This is strategically important if women are not to be relegated to a subordinate position. Women are the primary group to whom lesbian feminists are committed. The patriarchal structures and models of relating are rejected. Instead, opportunities are created for women to strengthen their commitment to women and provide a complete political analysis of women's oppression. This enables the creation of conditions under which power based relations can be eliminated, thereby allowing the growth of a new non-oppressive order.[49] Lesbian feminism is not

---

47 *In spite of this wish, reality does not always live up to our political ideals. That does not mean that we should give up our ideals.*

48 *Adrienne Rich in 1981 wrote: '.. we can say that there is a nascent feminist political content in the act of choosing a woman lover or life partner in the face of institutionalized heterosexuality. But for lesbian existence to realize this political content in an ultimately liberating form, the erotic choice must depend and expand into conscious woman-identification — into lesbian/ feminism' (Rich 1981, p. 31).*

49 *This is a short discussion of why lesbian feminism is important to the attainment of goals sought by the women's liberation movement. I have*

inconsistent with women deciding the remain single, indeed it often allows women to release themselves from the demands of patriarchal relationships and enables women to forge new paths in their lives.

3.3 Critiques of Separatism and Responses

There are three main criticisms of separatism that I answer here.

1. Separatism is a manifestation of sexism
Mihailo Markovic expresses this one vehemently. He claims that the women's movement restricts possible allies by

> ... a specific form of sexism, a female chauvinism that consists in expressing resentment, hostility and even hatred for the opposite sex, urging women from the movement to have sexual relationships only with other women. Now every individual must be free to choose the most suitable form of her/his sexual life and at the same time must respect the freedom of others. Thus the same principle that supports the rights to be lesbian also obliges one to respect the right of others to be heterosexual. To violate this principle means both to severely restrict individual freedom within the movement and to alienate male supports outside it (Markovic 1973–74, p. 165).

---

continued to write about these issues since 1976. See Hawthorne 2003; 2007c; 2010.

Sexism is the institutionalised discrimination of persons on the basis of sex alone. Women have been the subjects of sexism and because this has resulted in widespread inequality in relations between women and men, women withdrawing from such relations or limiting the amount of contact they have with men is not sexist. That is, there are no legal ramifications for men if women practise separatism. Sexism, as practised by men, is institutionalised. Separatism is one way in which women can minimise the extent to which men can exercise sexist power over women.

To follow this up on a slightly different tack, it can be argued that an oppressed group, in order to achieve liberation, must prevent the oppressors from engaging in oppressive activity. Separatism is one way of minimising the amount of oppression which women face in this society in most relations with men, and thus can create an effective basis for political activity on the part of women to achieve liberation.

As Markovic claims this may restrict the *number* of possible allies, but it may also increase the *effectiveness* of political action.

Markovic's reply that all individuals have the 'right to choose the most suitable form of her/his sexual life' is an important point. And I agree with it. However, at this time all people do not have that choice.[50] Legitimate relations between people are

---

50　*Markovic's claim, however, smacks of libertarianism rather than liberation. Through his statement he potentially allows violence, pornography, BDSM and other practices that do not enhance women's pathways to autonomy and liberation. In 1976, I was not familiar with the libertarian stance which was only to appear in a major way some years after writing this text. See Leidholdt and Raymond 1990; Hawthorne 1992.*

restricted to heterosexual relations[51] and though some people do step outside that mode it cannot be definitely claimed that those who remain within it do so by choice.[52] Markovic uses heterosexuality as the norm against which he measures the extent of a person's freedom, using as his basis an institution that allows little freedom of choice. He is unaware that it is the institution and ideology of heterosexuality that lesbian feminism criticises. The institutionalised inequalities will have to be eliminated before any people can claim to be liberated.

Virginia Held rejects separatism on the grounds that

> ... if one seeks the transformation of society into a community of equals ... separatism is not ... an answer ... if women refuse to let themselves love men, they betray the goal of a society in which power is not the ultimate arbiter (Held cited in Ketchum and Pierce 1975, p. 13).

But when the differential in power between women and men works to limit women's access to, and exercise of, power — while having the opposite effect with regard to men — then the chance

---

51 *Legitimate relations are those recognised by law. Heterosexuality was definitely the only legitimate sexual relation in 1976. With changes to marriage laws and others such as inheritance, medical attorney and the like, the level of legitimacy in some countries has changed.*

52 *In 1981 Adrienne Rich in her famous essay* Compulsory Heterosexuality and Lesbian Existence *wrote:*
Lesbian existence comprises not only the breaking of a taboo and the rejection of a compulsory way of life. It is also a direct or indirect attack on male right of access to women. But it is more than these, although we may first begin to perceive it as a form of nay-saying to patriarchy, an act of resistance (Rich 1981, p. 21).

of 'a community of equals' developing within a system that endorses inequality are very slight.

2. The second criticism made of separatism is twofold

2a. Separatism is essentially an ineffective strategy because not all women will or will want to partake of it; and a subsidiary claim;

2b. Separatism is counter productive and counter cultural.

An explication of 2a has been put forward in a paper "Women's Liberation: The Problems and Potential" where it is stated that

> [S]eparatism is not a political reality because women must eat and work and have shelter and they do have children. Furthermore it is inherently a romantic or idealistic red herring, because all women will never leave the system or stop relating to men ... therefore the selfish solution of let's get together and do our own thing or look after ourselves does not express a commitment to all women and children (or people) but a rather short-sighted commitment to oneself (Wishart *et al.* 1976, p. 7).

Using separatism as a strategy does not mean that women who choose it will stop working for and with other women who are not separatists,[53] but it does mean that they are not prepared to

---

53 *The support is generally lacking in the other direction: lesbians have been responsible for working on behalf of all women including heterosexual women and their children facing violence from men, heterosexual women used as guinea pigs in medical experimentation and on behalf of women exploited by pimps and pornographers (among many other areas). Lesbians have also supported gay men, especially during the AIDS crisis of the 1990s. I am yet to see a major campaign of support specifically for lesbians such as those suffering corrective rape or torture organised by heterosexual women*

work for the benefit of men, nor to support men, any longer. By not relating with men conflict may be lessened, thus expenditure of energy will be reduced and lead to more questioning of the heterosexist nature of patriarchal society.

Separatist women are not just removing themselves from the rest of society in an apolitical way. Separatism is a political strategy used to change society. We all contribute to the forms society takes and if our actions are backed by a political analysis and there is consistency between the analysis and our actions then, up to a point, the form society takes can be directed with the possibility that that which is created with new assumptions will eventuate into something new and non-oppressive.

Separatism does not mean that women have no contact with men at all, but that the contact they do have is primarily not to support men but instead to support women, since supporting men increases men's access to power over women. By limiting the amount of time spent with men, indirectly at least more time and energy is available for fighting on behalf of women. Furthermore, as Ketchum and Pierce state, men '... might work faster if women pulled out on them' (1975, p. 15) especially in relationships, an area of life in which many men are emotionally crippled. This is so because patriarchy affects men too since emotions are seen as feminine and thus to be avoided if one is a man. But with women supporting men in this area they can on the whole afford to ignore their emotional lives. Men, in general, have too much to lose in terms of power if they do not

---

(or men) or by gay men. (See Hawthorne 2005a, 2005b, 2007b, 2009, 2011b). It is also the subject of my novel Dark Matters *(2017).*

concentrate on the 'more important' male traits. As Shulamith Firestone states, '... male culture is parasitical, feeding on the emotional strength of women without reciprocity' (Firestone 1972, p. 123).

Stronger proponents of separatism recommend — because of the above complications of supporting men — celibacy or lesbian existence as a strategy which has political significance. This is one form — and it is not the only form — but one way of women creating a new vision for the world and coping with the present as best as possible. The myth that lesbians are 'super feminists' is ill-founded because it is not possible to throw away all that one has learnt growing up in this male-dominated society in a very short time. Mutual relationships in our society are most likely between feminists. This does not mean that it is essential that all women become lesbians, or separatists, or both, but it does mean that this has to be considered carefully as a challenge to the institutions that support a male supremacist and heterosexist society.

2b. Separatism is counter productive and counter cultural

Separatism is not counter cultural. Counter culture is a sub-culture dominated by men who reject *some* of the values emphasised in our society. But on the whole they do not reject or question the institution of heterosexuality.

The charge that separatism is counter-revolutionary and counter productive comes from those who claim, like Held, that men will change if women are nice to them; or from those who think that separatism causes divisiveness between women because non-separatist women will be alienated from feminism and this therefore will decrease the effectiveness of feminism.

I have dealt with the former above in my comments about Wishart *et al* (1976) and so will not defend it further here.[54] The reason for the claim that separatism causes divisiveness is not entirely clear, but I suggest that it is due to the internalisation of oppressors' values.

Internalisation of the oppressors' values by women, results in the oppressed disparaging actions that are not supported in any way by the existing structures.[55] With regard to separatism, it is unlikely that men will support this as a strategy. Some women will also not support it. I have, however, at no stage advocated *complete* separatism for all women. Divisiveness arises when this is taken to be the position for which I am arguing. Some women will separate as much as is possible in this society. Others will not. What I am advocating is that most women be separatist in some aspects of their lives that are relevant to the goals of women's liberation. And as noted before, women's liberation has always encouraged separatism with consciousness-raising

---

54 *What has become clear in the decades that have passed since writing this text is that the greatest divisions have been created by male-centred and male-driven groups. Among them are Men's Rights Activists (MRAs), lesbian-hating transgender organisations, some queer-based Pride marches and individuals. Heterosexual feminists do defend lesbians and are far less likely to attack lesbians and separatists and radical feminists unless they are funded by a libertarian, right-wing or sex-industry body.*

55 *Examples of this would include making it illegal for lesbians to hold women-only (lesbian) events where women are defined as those born with female bodies (XX). The Intersex community, on the whole, is critical not of lesbians but of transgender groups who claim that the body is simply 'an identity'. The*

groups, activist groups and women's organisations set up by and for women.

Separatism leads to questioning of some fundamental[56] aspects of our lives. While those who accept those fundamentals as valid or given will feel threatened, this does not mean these values should not be challenged.

3. The third major criticism concerns the consistency of separatism seen within the context of feminist goals and the often assumed corollary, that separatism is a goal
I need to deal with this only briefly.

The most often stated goal of feminism is the liberation of all women and as a consequence the liberation of all men. Thus eventually *all* people will be affected. No group seeking liberation ever has as their primary commitment the liberation of the oppressor — the oppressors' liberation is a consequence that follows *if and only if* the oppressed first liberate themselves. Oppressed peoples (including those fighting wars of independence) have their own communities in which they can support each other, something that heterosexuality and marriage/partner relations politically often deprive women from having. So while at first, separatism seems inconsistent with the goal of liberation for all, it is in fact an important step towards this goal. Women working together are better able to

---

Michigan Womyn's Music Festival has been divided not by separatists but by transgender individuals who began life with male bodies (XY). A series of legal judgments in Australia has prevented lesbians from organising lesbian festivals.

56   See the discussion on Romantic Love, pp. 60–66.

achieve this than if they are separated from one another and working with and for the oppressor.

The usually fearful attack on separatism on the grounds that it is an end in itself depends on (1) the success of women as a political sex class and (2) on the subsequent success or failure of the liberation of men.

The liberation of men is not the responsibility of women, though it might be a consequence of women's liberation. If separatism is an effective way of supporting women to achieve liberation, then it will probably contribute to the liberation of others. Separatism will only be an end for women if relations between men and women remain oppressive no matter what the prevailing social structures are.

Finally, I will examine the underlying assumptions of separatism. Briefly, they concern:

1. the nature and quality of male/female relationships on all levels (social, political, economic, sexual).
2. The degree of changeability that one accepts as possible for all human beings.

I have dealt with both of these to some extent, so here I will consider them in relation to separatism.

Point 1 has two subsidiaries:

1a. that relations between men and women are oppressive in patriarchal societies
1b. that relations between women and women are not oppressive.

(1a) I have dealt with this in considerable detail and it is clear that if women are by definition oppressed by men/maleness in a patriarchy then relations based on power will be oppressive. Of course, there are degrees of oppression, (e.g. race and class) but the patriarchy operates to their advantage with or without their consent.

(1b) is not clear, but given our present social, political and economic situation it seems likely that relations between women (who are feminists) are most likely to be non-oppressive. I have dealt with this in section 3.1.

Oppression is possible in relationships between women, but it is the only relationship that has the potential to be non-oppressive in patriarchy, unless women have internalised patriarchal values.

That these assumptions hold, — i.e. (1a) and (1b) are important justifications for separatism as an 'interim' lifestyle and as a political strategy. I should point that the quality of relations affects the effectiveness of any activity which may lead to liberation.

The notion of change — and the acceptance that fundamental changes are possible — is integral to feminism. Environments and strategies that are conducive to such changes taking place are important. If men are capable of change, then it is a matter of political willpower that they too effect change in their lives. Women — through consciousness raising, political action and cultural creation — have brought such changes to their lives often through working with other women, i.e. through separatist action in some part of their life that is relevant to the goals of women's liberation. These have been considered an essential means of women coming to identify with other women as members of an oppressed political group. Separatism needs to be encouraged at this level. It is consistent with feminist goals, given the existing power structures, to advocate separatism on a broader basis as a political strategy.

Afterword

Having reached this point in my argument, some of you might have decided that I think all men are dangerous and that there is no hope for men under patriarchy. But at the core of my book is the thesis that humans *are* capable of change. Women have been undergoing that transformative process over the last five decades and in the decades and centuries before women have done the same. Feminism is transformative. The problem is that too many men and women have decided that feminism has nothing to do with them.

Feminism is all about change and transformation but you can't liberate another person; they have do it for themselves. You can, however, encourage, and you can point in the direction of some strategies. This book is about saying that women need their own spaces in order to discuss, to celebrate, to move on from trauma and be inventive about their future. Women will choose different paths: some will stay in heterosexual relationships even when they are not perfect, because they believe in the relationship; some will stay because of fear. If each of those women is able to find strength in their friendships with other women and they recognise the political import of that, I would call that separatism in action. In between that are the women who engage in other kinds of separatism: there are many avenues to use political engagements in ways that assist with increasing the freedoms of women wherever they live.

As mentioned earlier in the book, separatism is quite distinct from segregation because the impetus for it arises from those who need places to be safe or to recover, or simply to be able to express themselves in autonomous ways. It is not a strategy to be imposed by anyone on anyone. I have experienced the freedoms of creativity in women's circuses, in women's writing groups, in women's activist groups and in many other ways. It's time for men to engage in change and to not colonise women's hard fought-for spaces.[57]

In a time when the war against women is escalating,[58] women need to draw strength from one another. Some women will need — and want — to stay away from perpetrators or those who look like perpetrators: men. Rape victims suffer ongoing effects of trauma in ways that resemble the PTSD symptoms of soldiers or how Indigenous peoples suffer from transgenerational trauma of colonisation. (Herman 1992–2015; Atkinson 2002, Hawthorne 2005b)

---

57 *In his book* The End of Patriarchy, *Robert Jensen makes important arguments for why men should start to make changes in their own lives and how they might begin (Jensen 2016).*

58 *The Destroy The Joint Facebook page reports the number of dead women in Australia. 'Total of all women killed by violence in Australia in 2018: 71.' 31 have been killed in 2019 by the end of July.*
    See also Impact for Women, 2019; White Ribbon, 2019.
    On world statistics: It is estimated that of the 87,000 women who were intentionally killed in 2017 globally, more than half (50,000 — 58 per cent) were killed by intimate partners or family members, meaning that 137 women across the world are killed by a member of their own family every day. More than a third (30,000) of the women intentionally killed in 2017 were killed by their current or former intimate partner (UN Women, 2018).

In this war against women, some men have decided to escape from their compatriots who have become too dangerous for them because they are challenging the norms of masculinity. There are at least three options that could be taken by the escapees.

- One is to occupy the space of women but otherwise demand that things stay the same, that is men maintain their entitlement.
- A second is that they could cross the border and set up independent organisations to support their fellow challengers to build a new life.
- The third alternative is that men could read, listen to and watch to see what women do. They could offer support for the campaigns women run, and at the same time not try to take over those campaigns. They could support the women who take the lead on issues that most affect them.[59]

Men are as capable of change as women, but as the old joke about light bulbs goes, they have to want to change.

It's about developing a language to speak about the perception of the world when you inhabit a very different corner from what is portrayed in the mainstream.

African American writer, Toni Morrison, achieved this with her books. After her death on 5 August 2019, a great deal was written about her in the media. But she has been voicing her

---

59 *It is interesting how little media space is concerned with 'transmen'. Is it because their social conditioning is as women and furthermore, that 'transwomen' regard them as a sideline. See Krishnan, 2019.*

radical ideas for decades and her readers heard her. Many have not bothered to read her books because it's not about them.

In an article in *The Washington Post* by Stacia L. Brown, Toni Morrison said this about raising her sons as a single mother:

> "You didn't have to ask. Everybody, particularly those of us who were without ... controlling males in our lives," Morrison recalled. "It was a kind of singularity. That intimacy, that instinct, knowing exactly what a sister needed before she could even articulate it, was what was so important."
>
> She is explicit about the role of black female friendships in lightening our single-mothering load. In the community of other women, we find respite and, especially among those of us who are artists, we can create for one another the uninterrupted time to engage with our work.

When I started writing this text, I was a young feminist (24) trying to work out my position in the world. I had left my heterosexual life around 15 months earlier and as we so frequently discussed in meetings, in consciousness-raising groups and over coffee which strategies worked best, separatism was the one that leapt out at me as ignored in the literature. It took some searching to find the essays that had been published. Also, my approach was informed by my studies in history including, Revolutionary History (Mexico, Russia, China), African History (especially the wars of independence across the continent), Women's History (especially the struggle for suffrage in the UK and Australia). All of these areas of study gave me a sense of the importance of the oppressed working together in order to free themselves, or in the language we used: for liberation. Within a few years, I would also be learning about Australian Aboriginal cultures and the importance of Women's Business. In the twenty-first century, we have all seen the power of women supporting one another publicly: in #MeToo, even in the Oscars. These are acts of rebellion by women standing together in a way that reflects the importance of separatism as a strategy for liberation.

I recall two really important moments of insight. One where I was sitting in the bush at La Trobe University next to a rocky watercourse thinking about the year ahead and about my thesis. Suddenly, the word power came into my head and I realised that this was an important element I needed to know about.

The second was a moment in the car driving to university. I recall saying to my partner at the time, Sue Ivanyi, that being a feminist means that we assume that we can change and that men too can change. In later years I have rendered this as the optimism of feminism, because if we can't change then we are really stuck. No radical political force can create an agenda for the future without the possibility of change.

The character Kate in my novel *Dark Matters* is in existential pain as she considers the crimes that have been carried out against lesbians and the knowledge that hardly anyone knows. That these crimes will go unreported.

I cry. I cry for all. For all the women. For all the lesbians. I cry because no one cries for us. In Kampala and Chicago. We are shot and raped. We are thrown from the top floor of a high building in Teheran and Mecca. When they arrest us, they put us in cells with violent men who think nothing of having their own 'fun'. In Melbourne and on the Gold Coast, we are tossed from cars, rolled into a ditch. In Santiago we are imprisoned and put on the *parrilla*. In Buenos Aires they insist we accompany them to dinner outside the prison.

We are caught, used and banged away again at midnight. On the Western Cape they come for so many of us that even the media notices. But most of us remain hidden. There are few reports of the crimes against us. Fewer readers (Hawthorne 2017, p. 52).

It is time to listen to feminist discussions about freedom and rights, fairness and justice, dialogue instead of erasure. And to listen both to the experiences of lesbians who can see the world clearly because of the way that power is refracted in their lives, and to heterosexual women who have carved out separate spaces for themselves. Listen to old women who have been in the world a long time and know how it works. In turn, dialogue across generations is imperative. Listen to your own passions and set about changing the world for the better.

Bibliography

1976

Allegro, Peggy. 1975. 'The Strange and the Familiar: The evolutionary potential of lesbianism' in Covina and Galana (eds.) *The Lesbian Reader*. Oakland: Amazon Press.

Allen, Pamela. 1973. 'Free Space' in Anne Koedt, Ellen Levine and Anita Rapone (eds.) *Radical Feminism*. New York: Quadrangle/New York Times Book Co.

Atkinson, Ti-Grace. 1974. *Amazon Odyssey*. New York: Links Books.

Baker, Robert. 1975. '"Pricks" and "Chicks": A plea for "persons"' in Richard Wasserstrom (ed.) *Today's Moral Problems*. New York: Macmillan.

Benglis, Ingrid. 1973. *Combat in the Erogenous Zone: Writings on love, hate and sex*. London: Wild Wood House.

Bierstedt, Robert. 1970. 'An analysis of social power' in Marven E. Olsen (ed.) *Power in Societies*. New York: Macmillan.

Birkby, Phillis, Bertha Harris, Jill Johnston, Esther Newton and Jane Wyatt (eds.) 1973. *Amazon Expedition: A lesbian feminist anthology*. Washington, NJ: Times Change Press.

Bloch, Barbie and Kerryn Higgs. 1976. 'Beyond the Cliches: A reappraisal of feminism' *Scarlet Woman*, No. 3, Feb.

Blum, Larry, Marcia Homial, Judy Housmany and Naomi Scheman. 1973–74. 'Truism and Women's Oppression' *The Philosophical Forum*. Vol. V, No. 1–2.

Brown, Karen. 1976. 'Reassessing Basics' *Quest*. Vol. 2, No. 3.

Brown, Rita Mae. 1975. 'The Shape of Things to Come' in Myron and Bunch (eds.) *Lesbianism and the Women's Movement*. Baltimore: Diana Press.

Bunch, Charlotte. 1975. 'Self Definition and Political Survival' *Quest*, Vol. 1, No. 3.

--- 1975a. 'Lesbians in Revolt' in Nancy Myron and Charlotte Bunch (eds.) *Lesbianism and the Women's Movement*. Baltimore: Diana Press.

Burnis, Barbara in agreement with Kathy Barry, Terry Moore, Joann DeLor, Joann Parent, and Cate Stadelman. 1973. 'The Fourth World Manifesto' in Anne Koedt, Ellen Levine and Anita Rapone (eds.) *Radical Feminism*. New York: Quadrangle/New York Times Book Co.

Cassinelli, CW. 1970. 'Political Authority: Its exercise and possession' in Anthony de Crespigny, and Alan Wertheimer (eds.) *Contemporary Political Philosophy*. London: Nelson.

Covina, Gina and Laurel Galana. 1975. *The Lesbian Reader*. Oakland: Amazon Press.

Covina, Gina. 1975. 'Rosie Rightbrain's Exorcism/Invocation' in Gina Covina and Laurel Galana (eds.) *The Lesbian Reader*. Oakland: Amazon Press.

de Beauvoir, Simone. 1972. *The Second Sex*. London: Penguin Books.

de Crespigny, Anthony and Alan Wertheimer (eds.) 1970. *Contemporary Political Philosophy*. London: Nelson.

--- 1970a. 'Power and its Forms' in Anthony de Crespigny and Alan Wertheimer (eds.) *Contemporary Political Philosophy*. London: Nelson.

Dahrendorf, Ralph. 1970. 'Social Structures, Group Interests, and Conflict Groups' in Marvin E. Olsen (ed.) *Power in Society*. New York: Macmillan.

Delmar, Rosalind. 1973. 'Sexism, Capitalism and the Family' *Radical Philosophy* No. 4.

Dolkart, Jane and Nancy Harstok. 1975. 'Feminist Visions of the Future' *Quest,* Vol. 2, No. 1.

Dunbar, Roxanne. 1970. 'Female Liberation as the Basis for Social Revolution' in Robin Morgan (ed.) *Sisterhood is Powerful*. New York: Random House.

Elshtain, Jean. 1976. 'Alternatives to Individualism' *Quest,* Vol. 2, No. 3.

'The Feminists: A Political Organization to Annihilate Sex Roles' in Anne Koedt, Ellen Levine and Anita Rapone (eds.) *Radical Feminism*. New York: Quadrangle/New York Times Book Co.

Figes, Eva. 1972. *Patriarchal Attitudes*. London: Panther.

Firestone, Shulamith. 1972. *The Dialectics of Sex: The case for feminist revolution*. London: Paladin.

Freeman, Jo (ed.) 1975. *Women: A feminist perspective*. Palo Alto, CA: Mayfield Publishing Co.

Freire, Paulo. 1971. *Cultural Action for Freedom*. London: Penguin.

--- 1972. *Pedagogy of the Oppressed*. London: Penguin.

Gillespie, Dair L. 1975. 'Who Has the Power?' in Jo Freeman (ed.) *Women: A feminist perspective*. Palo Alto, CA: Mayfield Publishing Co.

Gornick, Vivian and Barbara K. Moran. 1971. *Woman in Sexist Society: Studies in power and powerlessness*. New York: Basic Books.

Gould, Carol C. 1973-74. 'Philosophy of Liberation and the Liberation of Philosophy' *The Philosophical Forum*, Vol. V, No. 1-2.

Greer, Germaine. 1972. *The Female Eunuch*. London: Paladin.

Held, Virginia. 1973-74. 'Marx, Sex and the Transformation of Society' *The Philosophical Forum*, Vol. V, No. 1-2.

Herschenberger, Ruth. 1969. 'Is Rape a Myth?' in Betty Roszak and Theodore Roszak (eds.) *Masculine/Feminine*. New York: Harper and Row.

Johnston, Jill. 1974. *Lesbian Nation: The feminist solution*. New York: Simon and Schuster.

Ketchum, Sara Ann and Christine Pierce. 1975. 'Sex Objects, Sexual Partners and Separatism' paper read at the August 1975 meeting on Philosophical Aspects of Feminism at the annual conference of the Australian National University Philosophy Society, Canberra.

Kirkpatrick, Jeanne J. 1974. *Political Woman*. New York: Basic Books.

Koedt, Anne, Ellen Levine and Anita Rapone (eds.) 1973. *Radical Feminism*. New York: Quadrangle/New York Times Book Co.

Koedt, Anne. 1973. 'The Myth of Vaginal Orgasm' in Anne Koedt, Ellen Levine and Anita Rapone (eds.) *Radical Feminism*. New York: Quadrangle/New York Times Book Co.

--- 1973. 'Lesbianism and feminism' in Anne Koedt, Ellen Levine and Anita Rapone (eds.) *Radical Feminism*. New York: Quadrangle/New York Times Book Co.

Kollias, Karen. 1975. 'Class Realities: Create a new power base' *Quest*, Vol. 1, No. 3.

--- 1976. 'Feminism in Action' *Quest*, Vol. 2, No. 3.

Kreps, Bonnie. 1973. 'Radical Feminism 1' in Anne Koedt, Ellen Levine and Anita Rapone (eds.) *Radical Feminism*. New York: Quadrangle/New York Times Book Co.

Lakoff, Robin. 1975. *Language and Woman's Place*. New York: Harper and Row.

Laudicina, Eleanor V. 1972-73. 'Toward New Forms of Liberation: A mildly utopian proposal' *Social Theory and Practice*, Vol. 2.

Lloyd, Dennis. 1970. *The Idea of Law*. London: Penguin.

Markovic, Mihailo. 1973-74. 'Women's Liberation and Human Liberation' *The Philosophical Forum*, Vol. V, No. 1-2.

Martin, Kay M. and Barbara Boorhies. 1975. *Female of the Species*. New York: Columbia University Press.

Medea, Andra and Kathleen Thompson. 1974. *Against Rape*. New York: Farrar, Straus and Giroux.

Medvec, Emily. 1974. 'Quest Perspective on Money, Fame and Power' *Quest*, Vol. 1, No. 2.

Mehrhof, Barbara and Pamela Kearon. 1973. 'Rape: An act of terror' in Anne Koedt, Ellen Levine and Anita Rapone (eds.) *Radical Feminism*. New York: Quadrangle/New York Times Book Co.

Millett, Kate. 1972. *Sexual Politics*. London: Abacus.

Morgan, Robin. 1970, *Sisterhood is Powerful*. New York: Random House.

--- 1970. 'Introduction: The women's revolution' in Robin Morgan (ed.) *Sisterhood is Powerful*. New York: Random House.

Mothersill, Mary. 1973. 'Notes on Feminism' *Monist*, Vol. 57.

Myron, Nancy and Charlotte Bunch (eds.) 1975. *Lesbianism and the Women's Movement*. Baltimore: Diana Press.

New York Radical Lesbians. 1974. 'Woman Identified Woman' in *Lesbians Speak Out*. Oakland, CA: Women's Press Collective.

O'Connor, Lynn. 1970. 'Male Dominance, the Nitty-Gritty of Oppression' in *It Ain't Me, Babe,* Issue 1, June 11-July 1, pp. 9-11.

Olsen, Marvin E. (ed.) 1970. *Power in Society*. New York: Macmillan.

Oppenheim, Felix E. 1970. *Dimensions of Freedom*. New York: St Martin's Press.

O'Sullivan, Christine. 1976. 'Consciousness, Status and Power' *Scarlet Woman*, No. 3.

O'Sullivan, Liz. 1976. 'Organizing for Impact' *Quest*, Vol. 2, No. 3.

Pappas, Dee Ann. 1970. 'On Being Natural' in Leslie B. Tanner (ed.) *Voices from Women's Liberation*. New York: Signet, New American Library.

Partridge, P.H. 1970. 'Some Notes on the Concept of Power' in Anthony de Crespigny, and Alan Wertheimer (eds.) *Contemporary Political Philosophy*. London: Nelson.

Peters, R.S. 1970. 'Authority' in Anthony de Crespigny and Alan Wertheimer (eds.) *Contemporary Political Philosophy*. London: Nelson.

Phelps, Linda. 1975. 'Patriarchy and Capitalism' *Quest*, Vol. 2, No. 2.

Pierce, Christine. 1971. 'Natural Law Language and Women' in Vivian Gornick and Barbara K. Moran (eds.) 1971. *Woman in Sexist Society: Studies in power and powerlessness*. New York: Basic Books.

Pringle, Rosemary and Ann Garrie. 1976. 'Labor in Power: A feminist approach' *Arena*, No. 41.

'Politics of the Ego: A manifesto for New York feminists' in Anne Koedt, Ellen Levine and Anita Rapone (eds.) *Radical Feminism*. New York: Quadrangle/New York Times Book Co.

The Purple September Staff. 1975. 'The Normative Status of Heterosexuality' in Nancy Myron and Charlotte Bunch (eds.) *Lesbianism and the Women's Movement*. Baltimore: Diana Press.

Rapaport, Elizabeth. 1973–74. 'On the Future of Love: Rousseau and radical feminists' *The Philosophical Forum*, Vol. V, No.1–2.

Raymond, Janice. 1975. 'The Illusion of Androgyny' *Quest*, Vol. 2, No. 1.

Reid, Coletta. 1975. 'Coming Out in the Women's Movement' in Nancy Myron and Charlotte Bunch (eds.) *Lesbianism and the Women's Movement*. Baltimore: Diana Press.

Rosenthal, Abigail L. 1973. 'Feminism without Contradictions' *Monist*, Vol. 57.

Rothschild, Joan. 1976. 'Taking Our Liberty Seriously' *Quest*, Vol. 2, No. 3.

Roszak, Betty and Theodore Roszak (eds.) 1969. *Masculine Feminine*. New York: Harper and Row.

Sheila, Ruth. 1972–73. 'A Serious Look at Consciousness Raising' *Social Theory and Practice*, Vol. 2.

Shelley, Martha. 1970. 'Notes of a Radical Lesbian' in Robin Morgan (ed.) *Sisterhood is Powerful*. New York: Random House.

Shulman, Alix. 1971. 'Organs and Orgasms' in Vivian Gornick and Barbara K. Moran (eds.) *Woman in Sexist Society: Studies in power and powerlessness*. New York: Basic Books.

Small, Margaret. 1975. 'Lesbians and the Class Position of Women' in Nancy Myron and Charlotte Bunch (eds.) *Lesbianism and the Women's Movement*. Baltimore: Diana Press.

Solanas, Valerie. 1970. 'The SCUM Manifesto' in Robin Morgan (ed.) *Sisterhood is Powerful*. New York: Random House.

Solomon, Barbara. 1975. 'Taking the Bullshit by the Horns' in Nancy Myron and Charlotte Bunch (eds.) *Lesbianism and the Women's Movement*. Baltimore: Diana Press.

Tanner, Leslie B. (ed.) 1970. *Voices from Women's Liberation*. New York: Signet, New American Library.

Tarrat, Barbara. 1975. 'I Dream in Female' in Gina Covina and Laurel Galana (eds.) *The Lesbian Reader*. Oakland: Amazon Press.

Trainchamps, Ethel. 1971. 'Our Sexist Language' in Vivian Gornick and Barbara K. Moran. *Women in Sexist Society*. New York: Basic Books.

Tormey, Judith. 1973-74. 'Exploitation, Oppression and Self Sacrifice' *Philosophical Forum*, Vol. 5, Nos. 1-2.

Tschneider, Loretta. 1975. 'Bisexuality' In Nancy Myron and Charlotte Bunch (eds.) *Lesbianism and the Women's Movement*. Baltimore: Diana Press.

Valeska, Lucia. 1975. 'The Future of Female Separatism' *Quest*, Vol. 2, No. 2.

Wishart, Barbara, Zelda D'Aprano, Joan Russell, Anna Cushan. 1976. 'Women's Liberation: The problems and the potential.' Paper presented at meeting at Women's Liberation House, Melbourne, November.

Weisstein, Naomi. 1973. 'Psychology Constructs the Female' in Anne Koedt, Ellen Levine and Anita Rapone (eds.) *Feminism*. New York: Quadrangle/New York Times Book Co.

Wittig, Monique. 1972. *The Guérillères*. London: Picador.

Wolff, Robert Paul. 1970. *In Defence of Anarchism*. New York: Harper and Row.

Weber, Max. 1970. 'The Types of Authority and Imperative Co-ordination' in Marvin E. Olsen (ed.) *Power in Society*. New York: Macmillan.

2019

Atkinson, Judy. 2002. *Trauma Trails, Recreating Song Lines: The transgenerational effects of trauma in Indigenous Australia*. Melbourne: Spinifex Press.

Barry, Kathleen. 1979. *Female Sexual Slavery*. New York: Avon Discus Books.

--- 1995. *The Prostitution of Sexuality: The Global Exploitation of Women*. New York: New York University Press.

Bindel, Julie. 2017. *The Pimping of Prostitution: Abolishing the sex work myth*. Mission Beach: Spinifex Press.

Brown, Stacia L. 2019. 'Toni Morrison taught me I didn't have to choose between art and motherhood' *The Essential Baby*. 8 August. <http://www.essentialbaby.com.au/news/celebrity-parents/toni-morrison-taught-me-that-i-didnt-have-to-choose-between-art-and-motherhood-20190808-h1gxfs?btis>

Brownmiller, Susan. 1976. *Against Our Will: Men, women and rape*. Harmondsworth: Penguin Books.

Destroy The Joint. 2019. <https://www.facebook.com/DestroyTheJoint/>

Dines, Gail. 2010. *Pornland: How porn has hijacked our sexuality*. Melbourne: Spinifex Press.

Duffy, Nick. 2018. 'Trans women are women' projected onto London landmark after Pride hijack controversy. Pink News, 11 July. <https://www.pinknews.co.uk/2018/07/11/trans-women-are-women-london-landmarks/>

Dworkin, Andrea. 1983. *Right Wing Women: The politics of domesticated females*. London: The Women's Press.

Ekman, Kajsa Ekis. 2013. *Being and Being Bought: Prostitution, surrogacy and the split self*. Melbourne: Spinifex Press.

Haden Elgin, Suzette. 1984. *Native Tongue*. New York: The Feminist Press.

Hawthorne, Susan. 1990. 'In Defence of Separatism' in Sneja Gunew (ed.) *A Reader in Feminist Knowledge*. London: Routledge. pp. 312–317.

--- 1992. 'What do lesbians want?' *Journal of Australian Lesbian Feminist Studies*. Vol. 1, No. 2.

--- 1993. *The Spinifex Quiz Book*.

--- 2002. *Wild Politics: Feminism, Globalisation and Bio/diversity*. Melbourne: Spinifex Press.

--- 2003. 'The Depoliticising of Lesbian Culture' *Hecate*, Vol. 29, No. 2, pp. 235–247.

--- 2005a. 'Ancient Hatred and Its Contemporary Manifestations: The Torture of Lesbians' *The Journal of Hate Studies*. Vol. 4. 33–58. Online at <http://guweb2.gonzaga.edu/againsthate/Journal4/04AncientHatred.pdf>

--- 2005b. 'How to Count the Unrecorded, Unremembered, Unnoticed: Are there lesbian refugees?' Conference on Hopes Fulfilled or Dreams Shattered. Centre for Refugee Research, UNSW, Sydney. 25 November.

--- 2007a. 'Heteropatriarchy: Globalisation, the institution of hetero-sexuality and lesbians' *Rain and Thunder,* Winter Solstice, December. Online: <http:/ www.feministagenda.org.au/IFS%20Papers/ Susan2.pdf>

--- 2007b. 'The Silences Between: Are lesbians irrelevant?' *Journal of International Women's Studies. Women's Bodies, Gender Analysis, and Feminist Politics at the Fórum Social Mundial. Vol 8. No 3 April, pp. 125–138. Online at* <http://www.bridgew.edu/SoAS/jiws/April07/ Hawthorne1.pdf> .

--- 2007c. 'The Aerial Lesbian Body: The politics of physical Expression' *Trivia: Voices of Feminism.* Vol. 6. <http://www.triviavoices.com/the-aerial-lesbian-body-the-politics-of-physical-expression.html>

--- 2007d. 'Men's Patriotic Wars against Women's Intimate Lives: Patriarchy, the institution of heterosexuality and patriotism' *African Safety Promotion: A Journal of Injury and Violence Prevention.* Vol 4. No 2, pp. 20–31.

--- 2009. 'Do Lesbians Have Human Rights?' *Sinister Wisdom* Winter 2008–09, Number 75, pp. 65–81.

--- 2010. 'Matrices' *Trivia: Voices of Feminism.* No. 11. *Are Lesbians Going Extinct?* <http://www.triviavoices.com/matrices.html>

--- 2011a. 'Capital and the crimes of pornographers: Free to lynch, exploit, rape and torture' in *Big Porn Inc.* Melinda Tankard Reist and Abigail Bray (eds.). Melbourne: Spinifex Press.

--- 2011b. 'Are All Lesbians Sex Mad? The Fight for Lesbians' Human Rights' <http://radicalhub.wordpress.com/2011/08/10/are-all-lesbians-sex-mad-the-fight-for-lesbians-human-rights/#more-2347>

--- 2016. 'How do you protect yourself from rape?' Caja de Resistencia. <http://cajaderesistencia.cc/caja-de-imprenta/caja1-numero1/ hawthorne/>

--- 2017. 'How do you protect yourself from rape?' in Michelle Hattingh. *I'm the Girl Who Was Raped.* Capetown: Modjaji Books; Toronto: Inanna; Melbourne: Spinifex Press.

--- 2017. *Dark Matters: A novel.* Mission Beach: Spinifex Press.

Herman, Judith. 1992/2015. *Trauma and Recovery: The aftermath of violence — from domestic abuse to political terror.* New York: Basic Books.

Hoagland, Sarah Lucia and Julia Penelope (eds.) 1988. *For Lesbians Only: A separatist anthology.* London: Onlywomen Press.

Impact for Women. 2019. <http://www.impactforwomen.org.au/australias-death-toll-2019.html>

Jeffreys, Sheila. 1997. *The Idea of Prostitution.* Melbourne: Spinifex Press.

--- 2011. *Anticlimax: A feminist perspective on the sexual revolution.* Melbourne: Spinifex Press.

Jensen, Robert. 2016. *The End of Patriarchy: Radical feminism for men.* Melbourne: Spinifex Press.

Lawford-Smith. 2019. 'Why some feminists oppose allowing people to choose their sex on birth certificates' The Conversation. 26 August. <http://theconversation.com/why-some-feminists-oppose-allowing-people-to-choose-their-sex-on-birth-certificates-121874>

Leidholdt, Dorchen and Janice G. Raymond (eds.) 1990. *The Sexual Liberals and the Attack on Feminism.* New York: Pergamon Press.

MacKinnon, Catharine. 2007. *Are Women Human?: And other international dialogues.* Cambridge, MA: Belknap Press.

Moran, Rachel. 2013. *Paid For: My journey through prostitution.* Melbourne: Spinifex Press.

Murphy, Meghan. 2018. 'Trans activism is excusing and advocating violence against women, and it's time to speak up' *Feminist Current.* 1 May. <https://www.feministcurrent.com/2018/05/01/trans-activism-become-centered-justifying-violence-women-time-allies-speak/>

--- 2019a. 'Why I'm Suing Twitter' *Quillette.* 26 February. <https://quillette.com/author/meghan-murphy/>

--- 2019b. 'Women warned you: Yaniv's human rights case is the inevitable result of gender identity ideology' *Feminist Current.* 18 July. <https://www.feministcurrent.com/2019/07/18/women-warned-you-yanivs-human-rights-tribunal-case-is-natural-result-of-gender-identity-ideology/>

Norma, Caroline and Melinda Tankard Reist (eds.) 2016. *Prostitution Narratives: Stories of survival in the sex trade.* Melbourne: Spinifex Press.

Raymond, Janice. 1979. *The Transsexual Empire*. London: The Women's Press.

--- 1986/2002. *A Passion for Friends: Toward a philosophy of female affection*. Melbourne: Spinifex Press.

--- 2013. *Not a Choice, Not a Job: Exposing the myths about prostitution and the global sex trade*. Melbourne: Spinifex Press.

Rich, Adrienne. 1981. *Compulsory Heterosexuality and Lesbian Existence*. London: Onlywomen Press.

Rowland, Robyn. 1996. 'Politics of Intimacy: Heterosexuality, love and power' in Diane Bell and Renate Klein (eds.) *Radically Speaking: Feminism reclaimed*. Melbourne: Spinifex Press.

Rowland, Robyn and Renate Klein. 1996. 'Radical Feminism: History, politics, action' in Diane Bell and Renate Klein (eds.) *Radically Speaking: Feminism reclaimed*. Melbourne: Spinifex Press.

Stark, Christine and Rebecca Whisnant. 2004. *Not For Sale: Feminists resisting prostitution and pornography*. Melbourne: Spinifex Press.

Stiglmayer, Alexandra (ed.) 1994. *Mass Rape: The war against women in Bosnia and Herzegovina*. Lincoln and London: University of Nebraska Press.

Tankard Reist, Melinda (ed.). 2009. *Getting Real: Challenging the sexualisation of girls*. Melbourne: Spinifex Press.

Tankard Reist, Melinda and Abigail Bray (eds.). 2011. *Big Porn Inc: Exposing the harms of the global pornography industry*. Melbourne: Spinifex Press.

UN Women. 2018. 'Facts and Figures: Ending violence against women' <http://www.unwomen.org/en/what-we-do/ending-violence-against-women/facts-and-figures>

White Ribbon. 2019. <https://www.whiteribbon.org.au/understand-domestic-violence/facts-violence-women/domestic-violence-statistics/>

If you would like to know more about Spinifex Press,
write to us for a free catalogue, visit our website
or email us for further information.
Spinifex Press
PO Box 105
Mission Beach QLD 4852
Australia
www.spinifexpress.com.au
women@spinifexpress.com.au